Just the Four of Us
A Memoir

Anne Bell Ball
With contributions by
JoEllen Bell Wilson

©Copyrighted, 2021, all rights reserved by Anne Bell Ball

Just the Four of Us
Published by Yawn's Publishing
2555 Marietta Hwy, Ste 103
Canton, GA 30114
www.yawnspublishing.com

All rights reserved. No part of this book may be reproduced or transmitted in any form, electronic or mechanical, including photocopying, recording, or data storage systems without the express written permission of the publisher, except for brief quotations in reviews and articles.

The information in this book has been taken from various sources and is presented with no guarantee of its accuracy. We assume no liability for the accuracy of the information presented.

Library of Congress Control Number: 2021917428

ISBN13: 978-1-954617-24-7

Printed in the United States

Additional copies of this work are available through Amazon, Barnes & Nobel Booksellers, Ingram Distributors, and Yawn's Books & More, Inc.

Dedication

This small book of memories is for my two precious children, David and Janet, without whom my grown-up life would never have been complete. What special gifts from God you both are! I love you.

Contents

1. Just the Four of Us   1
2. A Real Home at Last   9
3. Mad Dogs, Drunk Men,
   and Other Fearsome Things   21
4. Joelene: An Introduction   31
5. A Father's Training: A Lesson Deferred   43
6. Entertainment without Technology   51
7. Hard Work Never Hurt Anybody   61
8. A World Apart   69
9. Dust and Dirt and Obsolete Contraptions   79
10. Cousins   85
11. Sailor's Song   95
12. Opposites Really Do Attract   97
12. To Daddy   111
13. Is Convenience Worth the Cost?   113
14. In the Corners of My Mind   127
15. Singular Events: A New Well
    and Hog Killin' Time   139
16. Porches: Echoes of Home   147

JoEllen's Stories

Whippings   155
Reunions   159
Medicine   167

Appendix   171

Afterword . . .   187

All one can really leave one's children is what's inside their heads. Education, in other words, and not earthly possessions, is the ultimate legacy, the only thing that cannot be taken away.
  ~ Dr. Werner von Braun

Just the Four of Us

Twilight. Daddy's sleek black cows plod aimlessly about the barn lot, silently chewing their cuds, one occasionally bumping another with its lowered head but otherwise oblivious to its bovine companions. Apart from the others, our milk cow—a beautiful, light tan Jersey—stands aloof with her head up, ears alert to even the smallest disturbance of the quiet evening ritual. Her name is Babe, and she is our father's prize animal. Once or twice a week, it is not unusual to see the driver of a dusty pick-up slow down to admire her handsome features as he passes our barn-lot gate. If Daddy happens to be in the vicinity, the farmer in the truck usually stops, steps down from the driver's seat, props a foot on the running board, and comments on the "mighty fine-looking animal." The two converse a few moments about Babe's last calf or the premium sweet milk she provides our family every day. They may remark on the weather, the latest news from down at the Co-Op, and their respective crops of corn or cotton or soybeans before the visitor hoists himself into his truck, slams the door, and drives away. Daddy may gaze a moment at the tailgate of the retreating vehicle, then glancing at Babe, he is likely to raise his battered straw hat just enough to wipe away the sweat on his forehead with the red bandana he always keeps at the ready in the bib pocket of his worn overalls. Patting the white star in the center of Babe's silky head and grinning broadly, he silently returns to his work, a man not only content with, but always thankful for the life the good Lord has supplied.

    But tonight the work is over for another day, and Daddy is sitting barefoot on the front porch of our five-room, clapboard house that is situated just up the little rise from the barn. He has taken off his heavy work shoes and washed his feet in the foot-tub filled with fresh cool water he brought from the well for just this purpose before coming in for supper. He toted a second tub for his little girls' feet and leaves it sitting on the steps in the sunshine to warm after sloshing the dirty water from his own vessel out into the backyard. He has also changed out of his overalls into a pair of khaki pants and a faded, button-up patterned shirt. He keeps this set of clothes hanging on a nail hammered onto the back of the door of his and Mother's bedroom. When he retires for the night, he will hang them back up for tomorrow night. They go into the wash once a week. The frayed hems of the pants brush the tops of his bare feet as he rocks ever so slowly in one of the porch chairs with the yellow and white checked cushions Mother sewed from a piece of gingham she picked up on sale at Lay's dime store in Cartersville earlier in the spring.

Mother and JoEllen, my 12-year-old sister, are sitting on the porch swing, their laps covered in old newspapers that hold the green beans they are stringing. A dishpan on the floor receives the strung and broken beans as their fingers work with the precision that comes with years of practice. First, the top where the bean was attached to the vine is snapped off as close to the stem as possible; then the "string" is pulled down the side, the bottom of the bean is snapped off, and the string is pulled back up the other side; finally, the bean itself is broken into two or three pieces depending on its length, the ends and strings discarded on the newspapers in their laps. Their hands move in rhythm: snap, zip, snap, zip, snap, snap, snap. I am nine years old, not quite old enough yet to be expected to help with the beans every night, although Mother has begun teaching me the age-old process as she goes about the various steps involved in every summer's task of canning beans:

Pick, string and snap; wash, blanch, and pack in scalded jars; place in 14-quart canner and watch the pressure carefully until it reaches the precise temperature; remove jars from the canner, set on kitchen table to cool, and wait for lids to pop, indicating that outside rings can be removed and the product stored in the cellar for winter-time meals.

On this particular evening as twilight settles and darkness creeps in, I am sitting on the edge of the porch, dangling my bare feet over the side. The tab on one leg of my blue and white striped shorts has escaped the D-ring that holds it in place, and I am idly twisting the end around the index finger of my left hand. Lucky, our new black and white pup that Daddy says is a "fyce," is stretched out beside me so that he can get an ear scratch from my right hand.

As the twilight succumbs to evening darkness, Mother begins to hum one of her favorite tunes. When she reaches the chorus, her clear soprano enunciates the lyrics:

"I've got a mansion just over the hilltop /
in that fair land that will never
grow old. / And someday yonder, we will
never more wander / but walk
on streets that are purest gold."

Daddy's tenor joins in on the next verse, and JoEllen adds an elementary but developing alto. I sing along too. After "I've Got a Mansion," we sing JoEllen's favorite, "The Little Brown Church in the Wildwood." Then, we join Daddy as he begins "On Jordan's Stormy Banks I Stand." I'm fond of "Deep and Wide," so we sing several rounds of that one, Daddy and I making all the hand motions before ending with four stanzas of "Amazing Grace." Our voices blend as only family harmony can and drift out into the yard, echo across the pasture, and fill the deep pine woods with the melodies of an abiding faith.

As we finish the hymn, Daddy quietly urges us to our feet. "Time to get your jommers on, girls. Looks like it's gonna come up a little shower tomorrow, and I need to get that hay up and in the barn before it gets wet."

Then turning to JoEllen, he says teasingly, "Josie, I'm proud school ain't started yet. You think you can handle that little tractor the way I showed you last week? I'm gonna need you to drive for me."

Mother grabs the papers with the bean refuse before JoEllen dumps the whole kit and caboodle on the floor in her delight at the prospect of driving the rusty orange Allis Chalmers tractor.

"Yes, sir! Yes, sir! I can drive it!" she squeals and dances around the porch. Mother looks towards the sky with its few clouds and silent moon.

"Law, I hope it does rain!" she exclaims. "I'll swannie! I really had to glean this morning to get this little mess of beans. If it doesn't rain in the next day or two, I may not get any more this year. I counted when I was in the cellar this morning – I've only put up ninety-six quarts so far. I was hoping for at least eleven dozen to get us through the winter."

We eat green beans—white half-runners—at least once a day every day, three hundred and sixty-five days a year. From mid-June until August or early September, they are fresh from the garden; the rest of the year, they are from one of

Mother's shiny glass jars that she cans in the fourteen-quart canner at least once a week all summer long. Surprisingly, we never tire of green beans. I suppose we never really think of such things just as we never really think of the beauty that surrounds our small house in the valley with its spectacular view of the foothills of the Blue Ridge Mountains just beyond the pasture fence.

"Y'all make sure your feet are clean. Don't want to mess up your mama's white sheets," Daddy admonishes us with a wink as we all go inside where one lone light bulb hanging from a cord tied to the pull-chain illuminates our way. JoEllen and I dip our feet in the washtub on the back steps just outside the kitchen door and dry them with a rough, hand-sewn strip of cloth made from a flour sack that serves as a towel. Back inside, we take a last drink of water from the dipper hooked to the water bucket in the kitchen and make our way to one of the two bedrooms at the back of the house where we share a bed.

"Night-night," we all chorus as we settle in for our night's rest. We say our prayers, "Now I lay me down to sleep..." and add our "God blesses," and once again quiet reigns all around the little country house -- except for the crickets and katydids who joyfully sing their late summer lullabies for just the four of us.

The View from our Front Porch
Painting by Louise Garrett Gentry

A Real Home at Last

Mother and Daddy married in 1937. For the next fifteen years, they rented and farmed several pieces of land with broken-down tenant houses. Only once in those fifteen years did they leave farming for a different lifestyle. For some eight or nine months, they lived in a tiny house just south of what is now the Marietta town square. The house was owned by Joe Herren. He was the proprietor of the restaurant on Lucky Street in downtown Atlanta that bore his name. Daddy's job was to produce a garden and care for the animals—mostly pigs—that Mr. Herren grew for the restaurant's kitchen. Twice a day, Daddy drove his old truck to the back door of the establishment, picked up the "slop" from the kitchen, and returned to the house and lot where he fed and nurtured the pigs, milked the cows, tended the garden, and performed other rather menial tasks. Mother despised every minute that they were there. About all she ever said about the whole experience was that it was a horrible mistake.

Daddy didn't like this kind of tenancy either, so after a short time, they moved back to Bartow County and rented the old Hawkins place with its sixty-odd acres of cotton fields. The house sat about three feet off the ground on rickety brick piers. The wooden floors were splintered and had cracks through which the dirt below was visible in more than one or two places. Walls and doors were thin and allowed the heat to penetrate in summer and the cold wind to whip through the four rooms in winter. JoEllen was born during the first summer that our parents lived on the Hawkins place, and she nearly died with pneumonia during her first winter there. From Mother's occasional comments about it, I believe that she thought she had "jumped out of the frying pan and into the fire" when she and Daddy moved from Marietta to the Hawkins' place.

A year later, Daddy struck a deal with a man named Aubrey Yancey. They agreed to farm Mr. Yancey's land "on the halves." Daddy did all the work; Mr. Yancy owned all the land. From the First National Bank in Cartersville, Daddy borrowed the money necessary to fertilize and plant the red clay fields with cotton; Mr. Yancy drove by most days to survey the progress of the crop. During the spring, summer, and early fall, Daddy hoed, chopped, picked, and took the cotton to the gin to be baled. Mr. Yancy got half the proceeds from the sale of those bales; Daddy used his half to pay off his loans so that he could borrow again in the spring. Of course, he also tucked a little away so that he could buy his girls new shoes for the opening of school in the fall. I was born during the second of the seven years that Daddy was a share-cropper. If Daddy ever thought he got the short end of the stick with Mr. Yancey, I never heard him voice it.

In the fall of 1952, Mother and Daddy signed the last of the papers granting them a loan of $85,000 to purchase the Gaines' home place situated about three miles west of the community of White, Georgia. The purchase included a five-room house, a barn, a couple of outbuildings, a storm cellar, and 182 acres of pasture and tillable soil. The place was both a blessing and a curse. In a moment of inspiration, Mother decided our farm needed a name and christened it *Sunrise Valley*. It was (and still is) beautifully situated in a little valley with a magnificent view of the Blue Ridge Mountains. Each morning, the brilliant sun rises behind those dark blue mountains and warms the earth for another day.

At last, our parents had a home and farm of their own. But what a house and what a farm they were! The original Gaines house had been destroyed in a tornado in the late thirties, but Mr. Gaines had built his four-room house back in the same spot. The two front rooms were a bedroom and a living room. A kitchen and another bedroom made up the two rooms at the rear. The house was a not-so-perfect square, each room being twelve feet long by eleven feet wide, and each had a door opening into the adjacent two rooms.

All four of the rooms also had an outside door in order to make a quick run to the storm cellar out back in the event of another tornado. The living room and front bedroom had back-to-back fireplaces that served as the family's only heat source other than the wood cook stove in the kitchen.

In the fifties, the Gaines' son, Marvin, built a new kitchen onto the original house. He attached it to the right side of the original living room, giving the four-square structure an L-shape. To say that Marvin was not a carpenter is an immense understatement. None of the walls in the new kitchen were square, the floor slanted downhill, and the salvaged back door did not match the jamb, so it had to be fastened with a leather strap to keep it closed. One end of the strap was nailed to the door. The other end had a slit that went over a large wooden spool he nailed to the jamb. When the leather stretched enough to keep the door from closing properly and allowing too much cold air to seep through the crack, he simply un-nailed the strap, cut it off a bit, and nailed it back. (American ingenuity never disappoints!) The door had no screen, so in summer when kitchen heat demanded that the door be left open, flies filled the room from early morning until late afternoon when it became so hot that even the flies made their get-away.

The original living room next to the new kitchen was turned into a dining room, and the front bedroom became our living room. The fireplace opening was closed off and a flue was added to the chimney near the ceiling to accommodate the smoke from the black iron heater that, in winter, warmed the three front rooms—living, dining, and new kitchen.

When we moved in, the kitchen contained a waist-high counter running the full length of the east wall. In the center of this wall was a double window, also with no screen. The counter was little more than a crude shelf covered in a maroon-colored piece of old linoleum flooring that had grown sticky with age. It had a sink suspended in the middle beneath the window; the drainpipe below the sink had an attached elbow so that it curved and ran through the outside wall, then emptied into the front yard where it eventually dissipated when warmed by the morning sun. There was one lower shelf on the right side of the sink. The slop bucket was kept on the floor on the left side; the water bucket and dipper occupied the space on the sticky maroon counter above the slop bucket. Mother and Daddy added their own wood-burning cook stove, a refrigerator, and a small metal-topped table with four Windsor-back wooden chairs.

Once the closing papers on the farm were signed, the kitchen was Mother's first priority. Daddy added a couple more lower shelves, and Mother made a curtain from dyed flour sacks that she hung from the edge of the counter to hide the pots and pans and slop bucket beneath. Somewhere, she and Daddy got the money to buy a new linoleum rug for the floor. It was beige and white, and there was enough of it to cut off a 22-inch wide strip which Daddy nailed over the old maroon piece on the counter. Voila! We had a matching kitchen floor and countertop! And, it wasn't sticky!

The floors in the other four rooms were wood but not real hardwood. Instead, Marvin had used worn lumber, some with splinters that really hurt when they came in contact with bare feet. In the corners of each room, he had drilled small holes so that the mop water could exit and run under the house, allowing the floor to dry more quickly. There was one closet in the entire house; it was about four feet wide and less than two feet deep and was situated on the right side of the fireplace in the dining room. We kept our winter coats, a few extra shoes, and a box for old newspapers in this closet. The two back rooms that the Gaines family occupied as bedrooms continued as sleeping quarters, the one on the south for JoEllen and me, the one on the north (the former kitchen) for Mother and Daddy. The doors between all the rooms were home-made and had no handles or knobs. Instead, Marvin had used his trusty drill to bore a hole on the side of each one about midway down. The holes allowed occupants to poke a finger through and pull the door closed without squeezing the finger in the process. He had added a heavy piece of string above each hole, and the jambs had nails in just the right spots to wrap the strings around if a person wanted to shut and secure the door. In our parents' bedroom, Daddy built shelves on one end, and Mother used her New Home sewing machine to make long curtains so that the folded clothes they stored on the shelves were out of sight. Sunday clothes were kept on hangars suspended from nails behind the doors.

There was a front porch about twelve feet long and eight feet deep, one end of which was unusable due to rot. The other end had a really nice set of three stone steps with elevated sides for flower pots, easily the prettiest part of the entire house. The clapboard exterior had once been white, but when we first moved in, it had large areas where the paint had peeled, leaving exposed wood beneath. The roof was tin and rusted. In fact, several spots on the roof were rusted all the way through around nail holes and, of course, leaked like a sieve when it rained. Mother set wash pans, gallon jars, and an assortment of other utensils about the house to catch the rainwater until Daddy climbed up there and patched most of the places with hot tar, giving our rooftop a sort of polka-dot appearance.

About thirty yards or so beyond the rickety back porch with access from both the bedrooms, the Gaines' family had installed a storm cellar. Its door was precariously made of cast-off wood and tin so that anyone who opened it had to be very careful else a splinter or sharp piece of tin would penetrate the skin. JoEllen was positively convinced that one of us would end up with "lockjaw" because of such hazardous outbuildings. (JoEllen worried about anything and everything, especially when she was in charge of me.) A descent down seven earthen steps brought anyone who dared enter this underground shelter to a room about six feet square and totally, completely, absolutely dark. A kerosene lantern could be lit to provide a stingy amount of light, but then there were the spider webs – great tangled masses of brown stuff that seemed to grab us around the ears and across the shoulders. The musty smell was powerful, and it was always a relief to scamper up the steps and back to daylight. Eventually, Daddy cleaned the place up, installed shelves (also of discarded pieces of wood, most of which were warped), and Mother made the cellar her domain. There, she stored her canned goods, and later on when we got into the chicken business, she sat in that cellar for hours on a little three legged stool and prepared eggs for market by weighing each one on a small scale, cleaning any refuge off the shell, and packing the eggs in cardboard cartons.

The smokehouse was just about as bad as the cellar and smelled mightily of salt pork and kerosene. A narrow path led between these two structures to a much smaller one, our outdoor toilet. Going to that toilet was a real adventure, especially in the summer time. We never knew when we might happen upon a little brown yard snake called a *spreading adder* because when frightened, it would spread its neck much like the poisonous cobra of Africa. This little creature was harmless, but you would never know it if you judged by the screams JoEllen and I emitted when one crossed our path.

During the next dozen years, Daddy cleared the underbrush around the outbuildings, managed to get a little grass growing in the yard, and built two chicken houses all by himself. Like Mr. Gaines before him, Daddy was not skilled as a carpenter, so the chicken houses listed a bit to the left, and the doors didn't quite meet their respective jambs. Nevertheless, they passed inspection by the county agent, and we were in the chicken business: a tiresome, smelly, unprofitable venture for the entire family. The four of us filled watering jars and feed troughs each time the 250 baby chicks arrived. Then, as they grew into laying hens, the jars were replaced with three-gallon buckets, and feed was poured into longer troughs along the outside walls. Twice a day, we emptied the inch or two of water left in the buckets, rinsed out the smelly sludge, refilled the heavy containers at the outside spigot, and toted them back into the chicken house, hens pecking at our ankles all the way. Perhaps the worst task of all came when it was time for the chickens to be sold. Huge trucks arrived in the middle of the night to collect the chickens we had caught by the legs as they roosted after dark. We had to shove them into slatted crates – three or four in each container – and then slam and latch the small opening through which they had passed. The ordeal left us with heavily scratched and lightly bleeding arms and hands from the spurs and beaks of the uncooperative birds.

    The day Daddy and Mother decided to get out of the chicken business and try their hand at something else was indeed a happy occasion. They mostly stuck to the back-breaking job of cotton production, probably because that is what they knew best. A few pigs were raised to slaughter, and a few more were sold for other provisions. Silver Queen corn was a staple crop, and during harvest, folks came from miles around to buy Daddy's prize produce. They also came to him for their corn because he was known to put in an extra four to six ears with each dozen in case the buyer came across a few that had gotten too mature to use. No one ever accused this man of being stingy! Once Daddy tried growing bell peppers, but apparently that enterprise did not turn out to be the cash crop he hoped for because it lasted only one season.

Despite the extremely difficult work involved, what Daddy most enjoyed growing and harvesting was cotton, and in the late 1940's to 1955 or so, the farmers of Bartow County, Georgia, produced some of the best medium-staple cotton in the world.*

The corn, the cotton, and the small black angus herd of cattle were about the only constants during our parents' lifetime together on this little piece of land, yet they always seemed content with their lot. In later years as they sat on the porch and talked, the day they recounted most often and that appeared to be their finest hour was the morning they signed the papers that granted them a place of their very own: a dusty, red-dirt farm and little five-room clapboard structure that they turned into a home for just the four of us.

*"The Cotton Story in Bartow County." Georgia Institute of Genetics, UGA Extension Service bulletin, 1952

Sunrise Valley Farm

**A Family Gathering at the Bell Place
(after renovations)**

The Barn

Mad Dogs, Drunk Men, and Other Fearsome Things

To say that our father was over-protective of his daughters is the understatement of the ages. Daddy was ever on the look-out for anything that might harm us in any way. Now farm life is inherently dangerous—for grown-ups as well as for children who follow along after their daddies, practically step for step. Farm equipment—especially the sort Daddy owned that was literally held together with baling wire and twine—can be the source of extreme injury. A disc from a cutting harrow can come loose and go flying through the air at any given moment. A tractor can overheat and burn a careless operator, or worse, can overturn, trapping the driver underneath. A plow can lose a shoe and cut anyone who happens to come along barefoot. The lever on a hay rake can slip and unexpectedly drop its tines to the ground, spearing the unlucky person who is not being careful. Outbuildings are not much safer. Daddy feared we might slip and fall from the barn loft; we could tumble into the well if we leaned over too far as we shouted into the depths and then listened for our echoes; we might somehow get trapped underneath the haystack and be unable to get ourselves out. Daddy also cautioned us to watch our step around the woodpile, in the edge of the woods, and on the path to the outdoor toilet lest we "get on a snake." We had to walk, not run, on the porch because we could fall off the end and break an arm. We could catch lightning bugs in the early summer darkness only if he or Mother watched us from the porch, and only he could use the hammer and a ten-penny nail to punch holes in the lids of the quart jars we used to collect the glowing insects. After all, if we did this small chore ourselves, we might miss the nail and hit our thumbs.

Our father hung swings for us way up on the limbs of shade trees and then warned us of the dangers of swinging too high. Once he built us a marvelous contraption called a Flying Jenny. In the late summer of that year, Daddy decided an oak tree in the back yard had to come down so that high winds would not cause it to fall on the house. He cut the tree but left the stump about three feet high. Then he got an eight or nine foot board, sanded it so that it was free of splinters, bored a hole in the middle, and attached it to the stump with an extra-large bolt. The board would then turn in a circle. The idea was for one of us to hold on to one end while the other held the opposite end. On the count of three, we would begin running, and when we got up enough speed, we would jump on the board, land on our stomachs, and take a thrilling ride! We were the envy of all our cousins who came to play on our terrific Flying Jenny. That is, until the day about three or four months later that Daddy observed how we sometimes jumped off too soon and risked getting our heads knocked off as the board kept swinging around. He disassembled the thing while we stood by and cried.

Whether it was Daddy's cautiousness, the fire-and-brimstone sermons we heard from the pulpit of Wofford's Cross Roads Baptist Church twice on Sundays and once in the middle of the week, or the numerous stories my sister read in any book or magazine she could get her hands on, JoEllen developed a keen sense of those things to be feared. Her vivid imagination took her places no one else dared go – except me, whom she dragged along by one hand as she skipped from one fearsome adventure to the next. Here is a partial description of the things we should fear most.

> 1. Mad Dogs. These animals are not pets that have been provoked to anger; they are beasts that have contracted rabies and go about the area foaming at the mouth looking for victims to infect -- according to JoEllen. If a person is bitten, he or she must endure – again, according to Jo-Ellen—a series of 140 painful shots in the stomach to ward off the disease and avoid an agonizing death. The story was told of

such a mad dog in the village of White when we lived there in a big, ramshackle, two-story house on the corner before our parents bought the Sunrise Valley farm. As the story goes, the dog's owner was Will Young, a local man often accused of public drunkenness though I never witnessed him in such a state. Whether or not the mad-dog story actually happened and whether or not it belonged to the infamous Will Young is not the point. JoEllen embellished this story with every re-telling, and Daddy was always the hero. One version had him shooting the dog between the eyes as it charged him. Another time, the dog was killed in mid-air as it leapt with bared teeth towards Daddy's exposed neck. Still another version had the thing sneaking up on him from the rear. Just in time, Daddy turned and shot it with his .22 rifle. What an imagination that girl had! And oh, how I loved being scared out of my wits by her tall tales of mad dogs and other fearsome things. Harper Lee's story of Atticus Finch and his encounter with the mad dog in *To Kill a Mockingbird* was published in 1960, long after we were little girls living in an old house in White, Georgia, but on my first reading, the tale was as familiar to me as the knuckles on my hands. I had heard it all before.

2.   Drunk Men. We always suspected that Daddy kept a pint jar of white lightning

in the barn for medicinal purposes, but we never once saw him take a drink of alcohol. We knew of others in our community, such as the aforementioned Will Young, and even a couple of our uncles on both sides of the family who were said to have a liking for beer and liquor. Daddy's oldest brother, Dick, was an alcoholic who reformed in his later years. JoEllen often spent the night with Uncle Dick and Aunt Evie (pronounced with short vowel sounds (EV-y, not EVE-y), and their seven kids: Katherine, Bobby, Alvin, Opal, Nancy, Andy, and Syble. It was not unusual at all for one of the two older children to leave in the middle of the night in Uncle Dick's old trunk to go to Cartersville to pick up their father who had been arrested for drunkenness. He was one of the sweetest men God ever created and never acted mean or disorderly, even when under the influence, so neither JoEllen nor I was afraid of him. JoEllen was, however, afraid of others who acted the least bit intoxicated or just looked like the type to her. On several different occasions, we were across the road from our house at Mr. Daniel's General Merchandise store when JoEllen would suddenly grab my hand and whisper, "Drunk man!" as she flew out the door, dragging me behind. I don't think we ever really encountered a person high on alcohol, but she firmly believed we just might and, like Daddy, was there to protect me from their possible misbehavior.

3.   Fast Cars. Jake Evans was a young man who lived about three or four miles from our house. He was the only son of a family with a little more financial success than the rest of us, and he owned his own car, probably a Ford. Every day after work, he had to pass our house on the way home. Inevitably, we would be in the front yard playing when JoEllen would hear him approaching. Yelling "Jake Evans! Jake Evans!" off she would go, running to Mother with you-know-who in tow. After we moved to the farm three miles west of White, she was still afraid of fast cars and cautioned me to never ride with our neighbor, Max Maybern, a boy a year older than I, because he drove much, much too fast. Ironically, she is now the fast driver. My mother once said that JoEllen had two speeds: fast and stop. Truer words were never spoken.

4.   Snakes. Big ones, little ones, fat ones, skinny ones, dead ones, and living ones. Snakes scare us to death! When we first moved to the farm, the path to the outdoor toilet was grown up and barely visible. Daddy cut back the weeds and a few of the saplings to make the going a little less treacherous, but there were still some dark spots along the way. Of course, the two of us always went to the toilet together to keep the other one safe. One time we were tromping along when I spied a little reddish coil at the roots of an old tree. Screaming as loudly as possible, I yelled, "Rattlesnake!" and we high-tailed it to the house. Mother took a hoe and went to see about our snake. It was one of those small, non-poisonous yard snakes called spreading adders that when frightened (as it surely was!), spreads its neck and hisses at the enemy. She promptly killed it and scolded us for being such scaredy cats. She spent several of her childhood years on a rocky little farm named Conner where real rattlesnakes made themselves at home almost anywhere they pleased; she had learned early that snakes are more afraid of people than people are of snakes and told us so. I still don't believe her. And neither does JoEllen.

Another time, Mother sent the two of us and a jar of cold water to the Three-Acre Field where Daddy was chopping cotton. On the way, we were singing and bouncing along as little girls do when JoEllen saw it: a huge, dark brown snake lying along the fence line with its head and about a third of its body stretched up on the barbed wire. Squealing for all she was worth and grabbing me, she hit the ground about every third or fourth step and ran as fast as her long legs would carry her towards our father who was within shouting distance and heard us coming. By the time we met, he was so scared that one of us was hurt that he had dropped his hoe and hat and could hardly get his breath from running so hard. Examining us and finding no injury, he finally succeeded in getting out our story: "A snake, a snake!" When he found it, it was a coach whip. Not caring for snakes any more than we did, he killed it and hung it up on the fence, a farmer's way of bringing rain to his crops. JoEllen's story? Coach whip snakes chase their victims and whip them to death! And I believed her every word.

There were a number of other things that we feared: black widow spiders in the cellar or, even worse, under the seat of the outdoor toilet; being struck by lightning while picking cotton; getting lockjaw from walking barefoot in the barn lot; contracting Rocky Mountain Spotted fever if bitten by a tick; being injured if the car slides into a ditch on a rainy day; and other real and imagined dangers. However, the most absurd fear was an outlandish idea that has stayed with both of us for all our lives and that still elicits a giggle whenever we reminisce about our childhood. When we were around 5 and 8 years old, JoEllen convinced me to hold on tightly to the back of the front seat of the car every time our family was in one of our old junk heaps --- just in case the car broke in half and the two of us were left behind in our back seat while Mother and Daddy went on in their half of the car to their destination! Only a little sister would believe such a preposterous suggestion, and only an older sister like mine could dream it up.

Being scared of "ghosts and goblins and things that go bump in the night" was never our problem. We were afraid of snakes and drunks, mad dogs and fast cars, and all the other perceived dangers that populated the world of our childhood in the rural countryside. Not much of true significance ever happened in our small community, but two little girls grew up there with a keen awareness of which way to run—and to whom—whenever fear grabbed our coattails and pushed us along to our next big adventure.

JoEllen and Anne Bell, 1949

Joelene: An Introduction

I don't know if young girls still have best friends that last a lifetime, but I do. Her name is Joelene. Not Jo-LEEN' (two syllables), but JO'-a-lene (three syllables). We grew up together – literally. Our families attended the same church, and our fathers were both farmers, so they were friends. Our mothers were in the Home Demonstration Club and Women's Missionary Society, and although they sat on different sides of Wofford's Cross Roads Baptist every Sunday, Mother and Goldie Lee Bishop (Joelene's mother) always found a few moments after church to say hello and catch up on the week's events--especially those that concerned their daughters--and to make sure it was all right if I went home from church with Joelene or if she went home with me for the afternoon. From the time we could walk until we graduated from college, not more than six or seven days passed without our being together. This is not an exaggeration; we were ALWAYS together; we completed each other and were just not quite ourselves when apart.

The first time Joelene came to play all day long, we were five or six years old. Her daddy dropped her off at our house in White to spend the entire day, not just the hour or two on Sundays that we had previously known. I clearly remember that she had long, dark braids that I thought were the most beautiful things I had ever seen, mainly because my hair was short, blond, and frizzy. We stayed outside most of that fall morning sliding down a small embankment in the side yard on pieces of cardboard that we had collected from Mr. Daniel's discarded heap behind his store across the road. At noon, Mother called us inside for lunch – turnip greens and cornbread! Joelene told me many years later that it was the first time she forced herself to try this Southern delicacy. As an adored only child, her parents rarely made her eat anything she wasn't sure she would like. I am sure my mother didn't insist that Joelene try those greens on her first visit to our house, but she says now that she did try a little bitty bite—just to be polite. She liked them and still does to this day. And no matter how much we try--and we both really, really try--neither of us can cook turnip greens quite like Mother's.

Jolene's mother died in 1984 from ovarian cancer. She was only 62, a stately brunette with light green eyes. She indulged Joelene and treated me like a daughter. She was also one of only a few mothers we knew back then who had a job outside the home. She first worked at EZ Mills, a cotton manufacturer in Cartersville. Later, she joined the sales staff at Sears. Her employment meant that she was able to save back enough money to buy some of the latest merchandise on the market for little girls. One purchase she made every Christmas was a new Madame Alexander doll for Joelene. We spent hours looking at those dolls through the cellophane window on their boxes. They were collector's items, not baby dolls to be played with. I never remember our taking them out or even thinking about doing so – they were special items to be cherished. Looking back now, I believe Joelene's mom bought these pretty dolls for us (yes, for both of us) in an attempt to add a bit of culture and refinement to our rather proletariat lives. She was always kind and thoughtful that way.

When we were in high school, Joelene got Weejun loafers, a London Fog raincoat, and Villager dresses, the most popular brands in the early 1960's. The dresses (made by Villager's sister brand Lady Bug) were paisley print or Dan River plaid with a shirtwaist and a full gathered skirt. They came with tiny red and black lady bugs pinned to the collar. Mother copied the pattern and made my dresses to look exactly like these store-bought affairs, and Joelene gave me a couple of her lady bugs to pin to the button-down collar. No one ever knew mine were home-made.

Joel Thomas Bishop was Joelene's father. We called him Joe Tom (behind his back, of course), but most people called him Joe Bishop—both names as if that were his given name. He was a small man, a tiny bit shorter than Goldie Lee, with a reserved quietness. Although he was a cotton farmer like Daddy, he never wore overalls. He always wore khaki pants and khaki shirts, both neatly pressed and clean. I don't know how he managed to run a farm and stay so clean because Daddy always had red dirt on his overalls, grease under his nails, and cotton lint or corn shuck remnants or bits of hay in his hair. Oh, how I wished my father looked more like Joelene's, especially on the rare occasions that the two of us rode into Cartersville with Daddy in his old junky truck, with him wearing those overalls! Joe Tom sometimes took Saturday afternoons off, something Daddy did about twice a year, once on July 4 and maybe another afternoon at laying-by time. Some Saturday afternoons, Joe Tom went to town alone to take care of farm business, leaving Joelene (and usually me, too), with Miss Fanny, his step-mother and the only mother he ever knew since his own died the day he was born. She was Joelene's grandmother in every way except bloodline. If it happened to be summertime, Joe Tom might spend a Saturday afternoon off sitting in his Ford Fairlane watching out for Joelene and me as we played in the Cartersville pool. What a treat that was for two little farm girls from White, Georgia! And what a dear he was to take us there on a hot summer day -- just because we asked him to. I am sure he had plenty of chores to do at home, but he rarely refused our requests to go to the pool. Every so often, he would also take us to Acworth Beach, a man-made white sandy shore on the banks of the Allatoona Lake. Joelene and I thought we were really big shots, especially since we got to put our clothes in a locker while we swam. Actually, Joelene did most of the swimming because she took swimming lessons. Bless her sweet heart, she tried her hardest to teach me to swim and dive as well as she. I never could.

Joelene has all the best characteristics of her parents, and they are innumerable. I will not list all of these wonderful qualities, but I can assure you, I see her parents in her every time we are together. She is loyal to a fault; she loves without condition; she sews beautifully; she is extremely intelligent; she's funny; she listens to others with attention; she adores her husband, her children, and grandchildren; she keeps her house spotless; she does not gossip – well, not too much.

When we were kids, we always sat together in church, either in the pew with her parents or in the one just in front of mine so that Daddy could thump us behind the ear if we whispered during services. Joelene had a keen sense of who was coming in the back door, and she would elbow me and whisper, "Now don't get tickled, Anne, but when you have a chance, sneak a peek at Aunt Katie's hair – it's purple in the back today because she was in a hurry when she applied her Fanciful rinse!"

Or maybe Joelene would notice that Miss Frankie had chipped nail polish. Miss Frankie was what we called an "old maid" although she was probably only in her 30's at the time. She and Corene--also an old maid and Daddy's twin sister--were friends and were also the only people we knew who regularly kept their nails polished. Joelene was always pointing out that her cousin Nora had better be careful or she would "plump up" like her mama (our Aunt Louise), or that Rev. Medford was probably going to preach too long and too loud again today. She usually had something to say about "Tootie" Kay, and it was usually funny so that I got tickled. Then she would start giggling too, and before we could get ourselves under control, Daddy would thump both of us behind our ears and give us a stern look. Ow! I still remember how that hurt. We even got the giggles when we were baptized because the water was so cold. I was shivering, but Joelene "helpfully" whispered that I would be even colder as soon as that water went up my dress and soaked my new panties. We "like to died" trying to keep our faces straight and serious for our baptizing.

  Going to summer camp is one of our fondest shared memories. Camp Wahsega in Dahlonega, Camp Rock Eagle in Eatonton, and Camp Fulton in Atlanta were all 4-H camps. Only Camp Fulton was free for us, a reward for some project we completed for the express purpose of getting to go to camp. I can't imagine now how my parents managed to get the money to send me to Wahsega and Rock Eagle. I wonder if the Bishops paid my way so that Joelene and I could be together. They were certainly generous in all the other ways they cared for me, so I wouldn't be surprised to learn that they helped out "just a bit" at camp time. We planned for camp the way people today plan vacations. Should we take four pairs of shorts or five? We agonized that the one swimsuit we each owned would not be sufficient although there was nothing we could do to get our parents to buy us a second suit. What if by some catastrophe we did not end up in the same cabin?! Which toiletry items were the most important and which ones could we share to save space in the one suitcase each of us was allowed? It was at camp that we learned to square dance and give public speeches; to sing in harmony and cook over an open fire; to jump off a small footbridge into very, very cold mountain water; and how to put on make-up by watching our cabin counselor apply her Avon. We also learned that we liked boys, and that some girls are jealous, especially of two friends from White, Georgia, who stayed together constantly, who made friends with other campers but allowed no one into their special friendship, not even Louis Barton, Joelene's camp boyfriend -- and eventually her husband.

When we were about 12, Joelene started cutting and styling my hair. Mother had always done this for me, but she was usually in a hurry, and my bangs were almost always crooked. Joelene solved this problem by cutting them short -- about one-inch long! When I looked in the mirror, I was mortified, but Joelene assured me that I looked great with my new "fringe bangs, the very latest thing," she said. Actually, they did grow back in a nice straight line, and she kept them trimmed regularly. She would also roll my freshly shampooed hair on her pink rollers to help straighten out the frizz. Of course, I shampooed her hair for her and poured on the Tame cream rinse that we mixed in a small glass – one cap full of rinse to one glass of water. Boy, did it smell good! And it made Joelene's dark hair extra shiny. I never cut her hair -- her mother had it cut at the beauty parlor in Cartersville--and we didn't dare mess with its length because Goldie Lee (remember -- we called our parents by their first names behind their backs) would have had a fit.

It was Goldie Lee who gave us permission to shave our legs for the first time. We were so nervous that we had trouble throwing our legs up and over the rim of the kitchen sink where we soaped them up before using her daddy's razor. What a mess we made – not just soap and water on the floor and cabinets but a fair amount of blood too. We didn't do any major damage, but we did have a lot of nicks, especially on our knees and on the ankle bones that stick out on each side. These nicks, however, looked minor compared to Joelene's upper lip the first time she decided to use Nair to remove the few dark hairs she imagined were growing there. Oh my! Red, red, red and chapped! And she had a date that night! We used almost a whole jar of Vaseline trying to repair the damage.

Strangely, as close as we were, we rarely had double-dates. My first boyfriend was Joel

"Satch" Holcomb. I was just 14 and he was 15. His sister Carlene and her boyfriend Bobby would let us go with them to the show (movie theater) in Cartersville. Joelene's first boyfriend was Steve Black. He was 16 and had his own car. Steve and Satch were not in the same class at Cass High and didn't have enough in common to associate with each other. But just because the four of us didn't go out together was no reason for Joelene and me to be in the dark about how each date went. The next day, we would recount our evenings to each other on the phone and giggle over our first chance to hold hands with a boy and our first tentative kisses, courtesy of Satch and Steve. Oh, we thought we were grown up even though our daddies still called us little girls.

I have tried to think of times that the two of us were "on the outs" with each other. There simply were no such times. In college, we were sometimes involved in friendships that did not include each other, but those were rare and short-lived and never caused an upset in our own relationship. As far as we were concerned, we were still the charter – and only – members of the "Anne and Joelene Club."

Almost seventy years have passed since that first day Joelene's daddy dropped her off at our house in White for our first all-day visit, and through all these years we have remained "best friends." Even when we have not talked to each other for weeks, if one of us calls the other, we can pick right up where we left off, still giggling and still sharing our innermost thoughts. Thank you, God, for my very special, forever friend.

Joelene Bishop, 1952

Joelene and Anne in Gatlinburg, TN, 1958

Joelene and Anne at 1964 New York World's Fair

Joelene Bishop Barton, 1966

Still the "Anne and Joelene Club," 2000

A Father's Training:
A Lesson Deferred

Someone once told me that the joy of writing a memoir is the ability to embellish the truth. My sister JoEllen says I must have embellished the truth or dreamed the whole thing up when she first read this story. She does not remember a thing about a particular summer evening some 60 years ago, but I can vividly recall the dirt and gravel parking lot, the small clapboard church in need of a good coat of white paint, the back pew where we sat for part of the service, and the big unfinished wooden box on the floor beside the pulpit. Daddy thought of this experience as one of those rural events the two of us ought to know about before we became the successful ladies he hoped we would someday prove to be. We had helped pick his cotton and had gone with him to the gin where it was turned into big white bales wrapped in brown burlap. We had learned to change a tire in case one of ours ever went flat, and we had been taught how to shoot his .30-06 rifle at a target. We learned enough about the Bible to win (or at least come in second or third) at most Bible School "sword drills" (see vocabulary section at the end of this book), and had witnessed a genuine hard-shell Baptist foot-washing service in which our own father was a participant. But this time, we were going to observe a faith practice that Daddy did not believe in but wanted us to see for ourselves as a part of our religious education.

Mother did not deign to accompany us on this particular jaunt into the rural countryside of Bartow County, but JoEllen was there -- even if she claims she wasn't. The late Sunday afternoon was one of those muggy days when dust coats the road, trees, grass, and front porch. It swirls a bit in the occasional breeze, but mostly the air is still with a rusty-red cloud hovering parallel to the earth, obscuring objects no more than thirty feet away. When we clamor into the old pick-up truck that will take us to the faith and healing service, the dust is our constant companion, and as we gain speed, it threatens to choke the three innocent travelers as we make our way along the back country roads.

As Daddy pulls into the churchyard and cuts the engine, he clears his throat, a signal that he is about to give us a short lecture on how we are to behave when we get inside.

"Now, girls, y'all need to know that these folks are very devoted to their kind of faith in the Good Lord. There is nothing at all wrong with them or with how they believe. It's just not the way we believe down at Cross Roads Baptist. When we get in there, we are going to sit near the back and as close to the door as we can get. And remember: 'Sit up straight and act like you've got good sense.' "

During this lecture, JoEllen is trying to ask questions, but Daddy is giving her "that look" that says for her to be still and wait until he is finished.

"You may hear some of the ladies mumbling things you can't understand – they call this speaking in tongues – we don't do that at Cross Roads either. Once in a while somebody may holler out real loud – you've heard Granny Bell shout at her church, so don't let that scare you. Now what I've really brought you out here to see is what is called the 'signs and wonders' part of the service. There is a place in the Bible that talks about having enough confidence in God that you can take up serpents, and they will not bite you." At this point, JoEllen is jumping up and down and I, of course, am considering a crying fit. I would run away, but there is nowhere to go except into the church or the woods, and I expect there are "serpents" in both places. I stick close to Daddy.

People are gathered outside, the men mostly in overalls and worn shoes, and the women and kids in flour-sack shirts and dresses. The mothers are shushing the barefoot children as all proceed up the open steps that lead directly into the church. There is no porch or alcove, and rude benches are placed from front to back with one aisle down the middle. Double-sashed windows are open to their fullest point and propped up with sticks. There is an electric fan and two microphones in the pulpit area – along with a large wooden box sitting on the floor.

We three hang back until most of the "regulars" are seated; then we find our places on the pew against the back wall. We are near the door. Daddy again instructs us to "sit up straight and act like we've got good sense," so we do. He also whispers that when he says, "Let's go," we need to make tracks for the door.

We are really surprised that we know all the hymns, and so we sing along, JoEllen trying out her alto, Daddy singing tenor, and me just being loud. So far, this is not much different from our own church revival meetings, except for the stifling heat and the odor of more than a few unwashed bodies. When the sermon begins, JoEllen and I sit up straight. We look at each other, and our eyebrows nearly hit the ceiling. This preacher is like the Holy Rollers at the church in White. After he utters a couple of words, he gives a deep "UH!" before continuing. ("And God said (UH!) Let there be light (UH!) And there was light (UH!)" We have watched preachers like this one get going on more than one occasion. The first time, our older cousin Wesley was visiting at our house in White and took us up to the vegetable garden that paralleled the road along about dusky dark. By lying on our stomachs between the rows of vegetables, we could peer in the back door of the Holiness church that was situated across the road from our garden. The worshippers inside could not see us, but we could see them quite clearly. In summer, that back door and all the windows, as well as the front door, stood open to allow a bit of air inside. It also allowed us to hear almost everything that went on among the congregation. We ventured out by ourselves a time or two after our first encounter at Wesley's lead, always noting loudly to our parents as we exited the house that we were going out to see if there were any lightning bugs. Even little girls knew that spying on church services – and even worse, giggling about what the participants were doing – was not within the realm of good behavior. Sometimes we saw a grown-up or two "get the spirit" and get down in the floor and roll around, hence the term Holy Rollers.

But today, we are both so caught up in our images of the Holy Rollers that it is a bit of a shock when we suddenly notice that the tempo of the service we are presently attending has risen to a fever pitch. The preacher is shouting into the microphone (this is a LITTLE church) and the congregation is swaying to and fro. Daddy has his arms gripped tightly around our shoulders and is blowing air into his cheeks and puffing it out at a rapid pace. All of a sudden, we hear the worshippers gasp, and Daddy pulls us to our feet. The preacher is holding the microphone in one hand and shouting down at the congregation. And in his other hand is a huge rattlesnake! He is urging others to "come on up (UH!) and prove your faith

(UH!)) by taking up this serpent (UH)!" We are out the door and into the truck in two shakes of a sheep's tail.

All of us sit quietly on the truck seat for a minute or two as we gulp in air and digest what we have just seen. Again, Daddy clears his throat, and again, JoEllen starts with the questions. I just sit there as close to Daddy as I can get and tremble.

"Why did that preacher pick up the snake, Daddy? Why didn't he get bit? Are the rest of those people going to get a snake out of that box too? What do snakes eat, Daddy? Is this a real church? We're not going to go back in there, are we, Daddy?" All this from JoEllen; I'm shaking too badly to utter a sound. Daddy is wiping his face with a bandana and licking his lips.

"You see, girls, not all folks worship God the same way. Now, I don't think this kind of proof is necessary. In fact, right now, I'm pretty dang sure the Good Lord doesn't need us to pick up any snakes. But what I want y'all to know is this: Just because we show our love for God in one way, it doesn't mean others have it wrong when they show their love for God in quite another way. I don't ever want to hear of either one of you making fun of the way people worship. And just so you know, that includes the "Holy Rollers" across the road from our house."

With that, he cranked the truck, and we headed home in a cloud of dust – still the same girls we were an hour ago, not comprehending then that our father was sharing a lesson about religious tolerance that would sustain us throughout our adult lives, a philosophy that has provided us with a kind of understanding for other faiths that few of our relatives and local acquaintances achieved. We certainly do not claim to be without prejudice, but we are both convinced that we are better, more sensitive women because of the many lessons Daddy felt compelled to share with his daughters, not the least of which was a trip to see the snake handlers.

JoEllen and Anne Bell, 1946

JoEllen Bell Wilson and Anne Bell Ball, 2019

Entertainment without Technology

In the almost seven decades that I have been a citizen of this planet, various and sundry kinds of entertainment have come and gone. Today, I sent a phone text to our youngest grandson to inquire about the current condition of his rather badly broken finger. When I first got a mobile phone -- the kind that rode in a saddle on the dashboard of my car and had a little mike stuck to the corner of the windshield --I didn't think I would ever learn to use the thing as a sub for my wired-in house phone, much less become one of those "cool" grandmothers who can send and receive text messages, take and deliver iPhone pictures, check my email, surf the web, and find out about the weather with the click of a few buttons. Being connected is the norm these days. Kids and adults alike run around with earplugs, iPads, DS's, iPhones, eReaders, iPods, and any number of other technological gizmos that most do not seem capable of doing without. Years ago, we never even dreamed of such wonders. We usually just entertained ourselves with whatever happened to be available at the time – if we had time for entertainment at all.

    Singing was one highly developed form of distraction from the day-to-day world of farm life. My family often went to a "singing" at a nearby church on Sunday afternoons. Sometimes, these events would include lunch before the singing actually started. Then about two o'clock, the pianist would get situated on a little round stool or, if lucky, a padded bench, and begin banging out some of the old familiar hymns to get the afternoon rolling. "Shall We Gather at the River," "Gimme that Ol' Time Religion," or "I'll Fly Away" would get folks in the mood to sing for the next several hours. Harmony was the mainstay of these gatherings, and the leader, who usually came from out of town to hold the singing, brought along some sheet music and some books (for sale, of course) so that participants could read their parts: soprano, alto, tenor, baritone, and bass. I cannot imagine what has happened to that beautiful, rich harmony that was once just the norm. The congregation at my home church now, Carrollton First Methodist, almost always sings in unison on the hymns and, if there is praise music, these are clearly meant to be performed in unison as well. But years ago, there were plenty of little churches whose members knew how to harmonize.

Quite a few of the song books and individual sheets of music that the leaders of Singing Schools had for sale had shaped notes. Lots of folks then (and some even now) can follow the melody by reading these symbols even if they do not know one single note of traditional music. Granny Bell, my paternal grandmother, was such a singer: she loved to sing "Fa-Sa-La" or Sacred Harp music as it has come to be called. Here again is that harmony that we just don't get to hear much of any more. I really miss that glorious sound.

In addition to church singings and Singing Schools, my family made several trips to the Atlanta Municipal Auditorium for what was billed as an "All Night Singing." We usually left the auditorium to return home by midnight, so I cannot attest to the accuracy of the advertising, but oh, what a time we had during those hours we spent on hard benches listening to such greats as Hovey Lister and the Statesmen Quartet, the Blackwood Brothers, the LaFevres, the Stamps, and the Chuck Wagon Gang. The four of us would sing all the way to the auditorium, most of the time we were inside, and then all the way home again, trying to sound like those we had just heard. On one of our trips, Daddy's twin sister Corene and her good friend Miss Frankie Sanford went with us. The next Sunday at church, Miss Frankie announced that the Bell family didn't need a radio because she knew for a fact that they could personally sing non-stop for at least seven hours.

I can still hear the echoes of Mother singing while she ironed, Daddy singing in the field, and, of course, the four of us singing on summer evenings on the front porch of the little house in Sunrise Valley. Surprisingly, however, we never performed as a family at church. Now, I wonder why we didn't since quite a few others did – and not as well as we could have! The Bagwell sisters, for example, were pretty regular with their "specials," but I saw a lot of eye-rolling and heard a lot of sighing every time they paraded up to the pulpit area to provide the offertory hymn or the anthem of the day. Maybe Mother and Daddy were afraid we might not sound as good from that lofty perch as we did in the confines of the car or out on the porch.

Although those days are gone, I still sing when I am doing housework or driving by myself. I enjoy the radio, and occasionally we go to a live concert, but somehow, the sound is not quite the same. I believe it is the lack of that old-fashioned five-part harmony.

We had other ways to entertain ourselves besides singing. Daddy once participated in a Womanless Wedding for charity. He was the most hilarious "bride" we had ever seen, stumbling around in Mother's high heels, "crying" into his lace hanky, and winking at the other guys in the audience as he tripped down the aisle. Both of our parents were always willing to be in a one-act play or bake for and participate in a cake walk or help with the Halloween carnival at school. Mother almost always entered her canned goods at the county fair and often won a ribbon at the Home Demonstration Dress Review for her outfits created from flour sacks. In her later years, she was invited to join the Cartersville Garden Club, and I know of nothing that pleased her more. Farm wives were not usually included in this prestigious group, but she became their chaplain and gained quite a few friends through her association with this club. Daddy held memberships in farm-related organizations such as the Co-Op, the Woodmen of the World, and the Cattlemen's Association. JoEllen and I joined school groups like the Tri-Hi-Y and Beta Club, and both of us were Cass High School cheerleaders, so we, too, had a few outlets for our spare-time energy. Even so, entertainment tended to be individualized, free, and sometimes just plain odd.

When she was eight years old, JoEllen talked Mother into allowing her to get a library card. Every time one of our parents even thought about going to town, JoEllen was right there begging to be dropped off at the library so she could check out several more books. When she didn't have new books, she read her old ones or old magazines or pattern books or billboards along the highway. Aloud. Over and Over. And over again.

I also remember punch boards. I am not sure where they came from, but someone in our acquaintance would show up with a little rectangular, heavy card-stock piece of paper with twelve squares. The object was to buy a square for a nickel, punch through the top layer of paper, peel it back, and see if you had won a camera or a pair of binoculars or maybe even a spider monkey. I never won any of those wonderful prizes. My punch always said "Try again." A better use for my nickel was the bucket candy at Mr. Daniel's General Merchandise. I particularly loved the candy orange slices. JoEllen preferred Mary Janes with the peanut butter centers and a crunchy taffy candy coating on the outside. Every day that we lived in the big house in White, Daddy would give us a nickel to go across the road and buy a treat. We thought we were rich beyond measure! And so did our cousins Linda, Lint, and Brenda Gail, and all the Bell siblings, especially Uncle Dick's kids. I don't know how our father managed to always have a few nickels in his pocket, but he always did.

Cousin Linda and I spent a great deal of our childhood together. We loved to play "Miss Woman." People these days call our game "Dollies," but we certainly never did. We dressed up in our mothers' old hats and shoes and were "Miss Women" for a while. We diapered our dolls, cooked rock-and-leaf-and-dirt meals for our pretend husbands, and rearranged our furniture. Sometimes, we used paper dolls. These little dolls were flat cardboard cut-outs that had several different outfits that we could cut out of the paper-doll book and use the little paper tabs on the shoulders and sides of the cut-out garment to attach the clothes to the doll. We got extra clothing for these paper dolls by cutting pictures of clothes we liked from the Sears and Roebuck catalog. Of course, they never really fit very well, but we didn't care and entertained ourselves for hours choosing clothes and dressing our make-believe characters.

Sometimes, we built a playhouse outside, an all-day project. Using a sharp stick, Linda and I drew outlines for our houses on the dirt driveway. These lines were enhanced with rocks collected from the ditches along the road. When complete, the playhouse had open spaces marking the doors and windows. We drew in furniture and appliances, all one-dimensional on the ground. It might take us the better part of a day to complete the playhouse, but that was the end goal. Once built, we rarely played in a single one.

Building pine bough huts in the woods or "riding" a tree sapling by pulling the green and willowy top down to ground level, climbing aboard, and pushing off the ground with our feet so that the sapling would spring back up in the air with at least one of us aboard was great fun, the sort of thing that every child who grew up in the rural South enjoyed. However, my best friend Joelene and I and first cousin Linda and I had two really odd pastimes.

Joelene and I really enjoyed playing Jackstones. Both of us were excellent, even when we got to "tens." We could bounce that little red ball, grab ten jackstones, and still manage to catch the ball before it bounced more than once. But playing jacks was just ordinary, something most of the girls we knew enjoyed. What we truly loved was cleaning house. Yes – we cleaned house for entertainment and loved it! First, we would go to

Joelene's house, a four-room dwelling with bricksiding (asbestos sheets made to look somewhat like real brick that was nailed over the clapboard). We would pick up any clutter and arrange it precisely on shelves or in drawers. Next, we would clean all the kitchen cabinets, removing the dishes and washing the insides and sometime replacing the shelf paper. Finally, we would polish the furniture, and end the day by mopping and waxing the linoleum floors. If we had a particularly sunny day, we might even haul the mattresses and pillows outside to air out. After sleeping overnight at Joelene's, we would get her daddy or mine to drive us to my house about three miles away, and then we would do the whole process again. Don't you know our mothers loved to have us entertain ourselves in such a productive way.

    Cleaning house for fun was indeed odd, but Linda and I invented an even more bizarre pastime. We shined bark. You know. We turned dull, ordinary pieces of bark from the trees in our yards to shiny, fit-to-be framed showpieces. Never heard of this pastime? Let me explain. First, we would gather the largest pieces of pine bark we could find. Then, using old newspaper and our own spit, we would shine the inside until we could almost see our reflections: spit on the bark, rub, rub, RUB the inside with wadded up newspaper, and then spit again and rub again. We placed these shiny pieces of bark all around our houses for décor. I can think of no earthly reason for shining bark, but at the time, we thought it was marvelous. In 2013, just before our 50th high school class reunion, Linda came to Georgia from her home in California, and I spent the night with her at her mother's house in White. We gossiped, we ate well, we laughed a lot, and we ended the perfect day by shining a little bark – just for old times' sake.

As someone has said, "In the old days, it didn't take much to entertain us!" I sometimes think my young grandsons need a lesson in entertaining themselves without modern-day technology. I wonder what interesting pastimes they might come up with if they just had the opportunity to dream, to imagine, to find something rare and wonderful that does not include a hand-held device that needs batteries and chargers. I am positive they could dream up something quite marvelous, but somehow, I don't think their imaginations would take them to the hall closet for a broom and mop or to the yard in search of the perfect piece of pine bark. And perhaps, that is as it should be -- each generation finding its own kind of fun and entertainment.

JoEllen and Anne with their dog Penney, 1948 or 49

Hard Work Never Hurt Anybody

We always thought that our mother was the first person to say that hard work never hurt anybody. Lord knows, she said it often enough. We heard it most in the fall at cotton-picking time when we used to pray that the school bus would break down, run in a ditch, or, at the very least, run late so that we would not have to grab a tea-cake for a snack, change our clothes as quickly as possible, and head to the cotton field, whining and complaining all the way with Mother insisting that all of us had to help, or we would never get the crop picked in time to get to the gin. And, after all, "Hard work never hurt anybody!" Now, it is absolutely true that this afternoon work did not hurt us -- we rarely finished a row by ourselves because Daddy would pick between us and pull most of our rows too. But that didn't really compute in our brains at the time. All we could think about was how hot it was, how heavy our pick sacks MIGHT get if we actually managed to fill them up, and how much the burrs on the bolls of cotton messed up our hands. We would start at one end of a row, pick about 20 feet, stand up, and look for the other end, declaring that we couldn't even see all the way to the stopping place. And when we got there, we had to turn around and pick our way back to the opposite end.

Pick sacks were available for purchase at most farm stores around Cartersville, but Mother made mine and JoEllen's out of fertilizer sacks. They barely reached the ground, so there was little danger of our hurting ourselves by working too hard. The store-bought ones that she and Daddy used were made of heavy, unbleached canvas with a wide strap that fit across the shoulder quite a bit like cross body handbags today. Of course, they were much longer. The sack itself began just below the waist and reached the ground in back. Most had "trains" that extended around two feet behind the wearer, and others were even longer. They had small rubber dots on the bottom so they would not wear through when they were dragged across the dirt as the picker walked along a row, filling the pick sack with raw cotton.

It was important that pickers wore long pants and long-sleeved shirts to avoid the deep scratches they would get from the cotton burrs. Of course, Daddy's arms were already banged up, so he wore short-sleeved chambray shirts (pronounced sham BREE, not cham BRAY) with his overalls. Mother, JoEllen, and I usually wore thin long-sleeved cotton blouses and long britches. The extra workers (called field hands) that Daddy sometimes managed to hire wore shorts and t-shirts. The field hands he used most often were the Woods kids from up the road: Eva Nell, her sister Louise, and their four brothers - Billy, Bobby, Johnny, and Marshall. Johnny often did not wear a shirt at all. These young people made our time in the cotton field much more pleasant. The boys argued all the time, especially about the Brooklyn Dodgers and the New York Yankees, and always had a funny story or two. They sometimes got into green cotton boll fights, and their aim was dead on. Johnny was the most gregarious of the bunch and was also the best shot with a boll. Marshall was the youngest and was in my class at school. He never talked to me in the field or at school. And I never talked to him.

All of these kids were great cotton-pickers. Eva Nell usually picked the most, often over 300 pounds in one day. By comparison, the most I ever picked on an all-day Saturday was 160 pounds. I don't think JoEllen ever broke 100. When Mother was not in the field with us to keep us straight, JoEllen spent a lot of her time asking Daddy if she could go to the house and get us all some cold water. He would let her go, but she would come back with red-rimmed eyes because Mother had shamed her and made her feel guilty for not doing her share of the work. Our mother was not a mean person; she just found this method worked great with her two daughters. Once JoEllen was back in the field, she would pick really hard for the next 30 minutes or so, but then she would need to go to the toilet. Lest you think I was slaving away, let me say here that I spent a lot of my time standing around while Daddy picked my row. I enjoyed watching what was happening with JoEllen. The only reason I got up to 160 pounds that one time was that I really wanted a new pair of blue jeans to wear to the county fair. Daddy paid us by the pound the same as he paid the Woods kids, so I had high hopes of earning myself a pair of Levi's with the leather label on the back near the belt loops. It didn't happen. The pay-per-pound of cotton was way too low -- around 10 to 11 cents-- or my sack was way too empty.

When pick sacks got full, they were emptied onto large square burlap sheets about 6 feet wide by 6 feet long. These sheets were stretched out on a cleared spot of dirt at the end of the cotton rows. At quitting time, they were closed for "weighing-up time." Two people, one on each corner, tied the cotton sheets by handing opposite ends of the burlap across the middle and making a large knot on top with a mighty pull. Then the two other corners were tied together in the same way, fashioning a somewhat rounded bundle.

Daddy called the balance beam scale used for weighing the sheets of cotton stillards. A large wicked-looking iron hook at the top of the set of the stillards was placed in the middle of a pole about 7 feet long. Below the hook was a heavy chain that dropped a couple of feet down and ended with another large iron hook. Welded between the two hooks was a hinged balance arm notched every inch or so with numbers that corresponded to a particular weight. The lower hook was placed inside the cotton sheet knot. Two men (or the two strongest boys) would lift the pole onto their shoulders and raise the stillards and the knotted sheet of cotton off the ground. Daddy would read out the weight as measured on the stillards as he moved various sized pieces of metal (called bells) into the notches on the arm until it rested level with the ground, thus balancing the stillard weights with the weight of the cotton. Mother's job was to write down the weight beside each person's name in a small tablet. She always bragged on how much the hands had picked and congratulated them for being the very best pickers in the county. JoEllen and I tried to sneak rocks into our sheets, but she always caught us and quietly removed the rocks, giving Daddy a grin as she did it and trying to look stern as she glanced at each of us. After the Woods kids, Daddy always had the next highest weight with Mother's sheet often coming in a close second to his. And then there were mine and JoEllen's -- PITIFUL! Clearly, we did not hurt ourselves with hard work.

  The very best part about growing up in a family that produced cotton was the trip to the gin. When Daddy decided he had enough raw cotton to be turned into a bale, he would load it on his old pick-up truck outfitted with homemade sideboards, load us on the top of the sweet-smelling harvest, and take off to Pine Log where the gin he used most of the time was located. Once we arrived, we usually had to get in line behind other farmers' trucks to reach our spot under the shed of the actual gin. There, a long, 12 to 15 inch-in-diameter suction hose dropped from the ceiling of the gin and directly above the truck bed. When the switch inside the gin was thrown, the raw cotton was sucked up and into the seeder housed in a room beside the shed with the hose. Someone had to stay in the bed of the truck to move the hose over the cotton, to get into the corners, and to make sure all of the raw material was vacuumed into the hose. JoEllen loved this job! She would sing while she worked, and more often than not, her straw hat went up the hose with the cotton. When all the seeds and other debris (including straw hats) were removed with the combs on the seeder, the smooth cotton fiber was fed through a contraption that packed it into a huge 400-500 pound rectangle called a bale, and finally covered in burlap. Daddy watched the price of cotton the way we now watch the stock market. His luck usually held to its pattern, and the very day he went to the gin, the price of cotton went down. I often wonder how he kept his sunny disposition and unwavering faith in God when so many of life's encounters left him wanting. No matter what, he never forgot to stop by Bradford's store in Pine Log on the way home from the gin so that JoEllen and I could get some penny candy. And so that he could discuss the miserable price of cotton with the other farmers who stopped by the store on the way back to their own places. This group of men didn't have much of a chance to socialize except at church and during brief moments at Bradford's store or the Co-Op, but their parting words still ring in my memory: "Say 'Hey' to your wife, and don't forget that all this hard work never hurt anybody!"

Emmett Bell in his Cotton Field

A World Apart

I don't remember much about the mid to late 1940's (birth to 5 years), and the sorts of things I remember about the 50's and early 60's are not the same as those you can read about in history books or on the internet. For instance, even though these decades are now known to have been the most turbulent of times for racial unrest, I was completely unaware that racial tension was even a "thing," and no one we knew participated in any marches, sit-ins, or other protests. The most important US Supreme Court case in the fight for racial equality, Brown v. the Topeka Board of Education, was filed in 1954, resulting in the landmark ruling that desegregated public schools. I was nine years old and in the third grade, but if my teacher, Mrs. Cochran, ever mentioned this important national news in our classroom, I don't remember it. And, I did not go to public school with African-American kids. In 1955, Rosa Parks refused to give up her seat on a Montgomery, Alabama, bus to a white person. I never knew about that far-reaching and monumental step in the civil rights movement until I enrolled in an American history class in college in 1964. The Freedom Riders of 1961 completely escaped my attention, and although I knew about Martin Luther King, Jr., and was stunned when he was assassinated, neither he nor his cause were frequent topics of conversation at our house, church, or social gatherings. Most of what I know of Dr. King's life and death is not a part of my memory bank; this knowledge came by way of the college classroom and through later television productions.

My ignorance of national affairs extended to more than the racial issues of the time. I don't remember President Truman's being in office (1945-53), and the only things I remember about his successor, President Eisenhower, are that his bald head was really shiny when he appeared on the television set we sometimes watched at Uncle Harry's house, and there was something about a pine tree on the Masters' Golf Course in Augusta that bothered the President beyond measure when he was in Georgia to play a round of golf. I was only vaguely aware of the 1950-1953 Korean War, the 1953 conviction and execution of the Rosenbergs for espionage against the United States, the ascension of Queen Elizabeth II to the throne of England, or the launch of the Russian satellite Sputnik in 1957.

The election of America's first Catholic President, John F. Kennedy, in 1960 was, however, an important part of my experience, perhaps because my parents could not imagine a Catholic Democrat in the White House, but mostly because Kennedy was such a handsome and charismatic man married to a beautiful and sophisticated woman. I also vividly recall the music of the mid 1950's to early 1960's, thanks to Atlanta radio station WQXI. Rock and Roll made its debut around 1955 with the voice and swiveling hips of Elvis Presley, whose raucous, often controversial sound was a combination of traditional country music with Rhythm and Blues. On the heels of Presley came such greats as Roy Orbison, Chubby Checker, and Buddy Holly. The most popular song of 1960 was "Rock Around the Clock" with Bill Haley and the Comets. By the time I graduated from Cass High School in 1963, the Beach Boys had made quite a splash throughout the nation with their sun-drenched lyrics of "Surfin' USA," and we were beginning to dance to the music of a little foursome from England named the Beatles. Aside from this music and "Camelot in the White House," I was practically oblivious to the changing world around me.

Perhaps the fact that we did not own a television until I was a sophomore in high school was a primary reason for my lack of knowledge about most current events, but more likely our family and friends just had other, more interesting things to do and to talk about.

Our life revolved around farm crops, animals, the garden, school, and, of course, the church. My first memories of Daddy's cotton crops are of the "red field" near the cemetery in

White. Daddy was a share-cropper when we lived in the big house in White (he said he farmed "on the halves"), and he planted, hoed, chopped, and picked the cotton in that field in the hottest weather imaginable. Mother, JoEllen (about 9), and I (about 6) would take him a quart jar of water in the early afternoon, and I vividly remember how red-faced he usually was and how his blue chambray shirt was completely wet from sweat. I also recall that he never, ever complained; instead, he would stop for a few minutes, tell us how much he " 'preciated" the water, and give JoEllen and me a wink to assure us he was OK before sending us on our way, often with a nickel to spend on bucket candy at Mr. Daniel's store. After our parents bought their farm three miles west of White, Daddy continued to grow cotton as his main cash crop – although I don't think there was a whole lot of cash to be made.

    Our farm animals were not like the animals that families own today. We didn't treat them like part of the family, except maybe our dog Lassie. She was originally named Carol by Brenda Gail whose dog Fluffy was Lassie's mother, but we thought the name Lassie was more appropriate. In addition to Lassie and our Persian cat Fluff, Daddy had cows and pigs, and he always had a workhorse or a mule or two. Scott and Charley were his favorite horses, but I believe they had to be sold before we bought Sunrise Valley because I don't remember having them there. I do, however, remember our mule Tobe. What a monster he was – at least he seemed to be one when I was small. He had slick coarse hair, a gray nose, and great big yellow teeth that he liked to show off. And oh my, was he stubborn! Daddy spent about as much time trying to control him as he did using him for plowing and other jobs around the place. When he got too old to work, he just ambled around the pasture acting like he was king of the hill. One day, maybe a day we had killed hogs, Daddy was taking him from the house to the barn with lots of "Gee, Tobe!" and "Haw, you old coot, Haw!" when old Tobe just killed over and died in the front yard! Daddy must have had his hands full with other tasks because he just left that old mule lying there the rest of the day. Tobe's belly swelled up, and he had begun to stink when some of the neighbors were enlisted to tie a log chain around him and help Daddy drag him over to the backside of the pasture where they rolled him in a hole that had been prepared for this purpose. That was one time that neither Jo-Ellen nor I cried when one of our animals passed away – we were not that fond of poor old Tobe.

    The way church business was taken care of during my growing up years was a good bit different from today, too. We were Baptists, and the preacher was "called" to our pulpit by a committee of deacons each time we were in need of a new pastor. Preachers did not have specific requirements, such as a certain amount of education or other credentials; instead, the committee went to hear him preach, and if they liked what they heard, they came back to the church conference, made their report, and "called" him to the pulpit for an unknown number of years. Some stayed two or three years while others were fixtures in the community for quite a long time. Most of the pastors did not resign -- they were asked to leave by vote of the church conference.

Church conference was a political arena. When a few members of the congregation grew tired of the pastor or had a complaint about some other workings of the church, they would "call a conference" to discuss the issue and make the decision about just what to do. There had to be a quorum present to make such decisions, and sometimes, the date and time of the "called conference" was known only to the group who wanted to make a change. We always went to conference, even JoEllen and I when we were children, and the talk could get rather heated when one entity of the membership wanted one thing while another wanted something else. My first experience in a Methodist Administrative Board meeting (the equivalent of conference) was a real shock. I answered to roll call, heard the reading of minutes from the last meeting, and learned all about Robert's Rules of Order. There were no raised voices and no arguments. This group of church folks had an agenda that they followed to the letter, and within an hour or so, the pastor pronounced the benediction, and we all went home, happy as larks that the business of the church was taken care of for another several months. And our pastor? This position could be filled by a man or a woman (certainly not the case at Cross Roads

Baptist) as long as he or she had a four-year seminary degree and maybe an MDiv and was a suitable match for the congregation in the eyes of the District Superintendent, the district cabinet, and the bishop of the North Georgia Conference. The church membership had very little say-so in the matter, but the good news was that pastors rarely stayed longer than four years. When they left, if we really liked them, we were happy they were getting a promotion; if we were not fond of them, we were happy to see them go. And we didn't have to have a called conference to make a change.

Socially, my childhood was very, very different from that of my grandchildren. Black children were not allowed to attend white schools, even after the 1954 desegregation law was passed. The first time I attended class with a black student was in 1965 at West Georgia College. Black children had their own elementary school, and Carver High School in Cartersville was there for any who could further their education. Many black people did not graduate from high school because they needed to go to work as soon as they turned 16 to help with the family finances. It never actually occurred to me (or to any of my friends, for that matter) that the races were separated. They just were. The courthouse had water fountains labeled "Whites Only" and "Blacks." Black people entered the movie theater through a back door and could sit only in the balcony. When Daddy hired a black man to help him in the field, he always called Daddy Mr. Bell or Mr. Emmett, but Daddy called him by his first name, even if he was much older. At lunch time, Mother supplied a meal, but these black field hands sat outside under a tree to eat, not in the house with us. Black high schools did not play white high school in any sports, they did not compete with each other in any competitions, and the achievements of black students were never written up in the local newspaper. While almost every white girl who became engaged had her picture in the paper, no blacks ever announced their weddings or funerals or any other event in the *Bartow Tribune*. Even retail stores separated the races. I cannot remember ever seeing a black person in a department store at the same time we were there. I don't know when or where they shopped. Looking back, I am truly appalled that I did not notice this inequality, but I did not. Times were different then, and we were a world apart.

Not all of my memories are happy ones, but as I have grown older (and maybe wiser), I readily acknowledge that it is so much easier to talk and write about the good times. When we cousins get together, there is plenty of laughter and very few tears. No one argues about what happened back in our childhood days. If one person remembers a story a little differently from another, we just smile and go on to another tale. My sincerest hope is that someday our children will find a time and place to gather with their own families and friends, perhaps some of them will be people of color, to share a "covered dish meal" and reminisce about those times in their childhoods that overflowed with happiness and joy and were set apart from the rest of the world.

**Sally Jo and Emmett Bell
Sunday Afternoon on the
Porch**

Dust and Dirt and Obsolete Contraptions

It is mid-July around 1954 or '55, the dog days of summer. Daddy has laid-by his crops and has parked his tractor by the smokehouse under the shade of the oak tree in the back yard where he is changing the valves or the spark plugs or otherwise tinkering with the old machine so that it will give him another season of labor in the field. Mother is inside ironing in front of the window fan and listening to her stories on the radio: "Pepper Young's Family" and "Lorenzo Jones," each of which lasts for fifteen minutes with most of the quarter-hour taken up with dramatic organ music and ads for various household products, especially soaps--hence the name, "soap operas." She gets time to hear these stories about once a month, but it is easy to keep up since very little happens in each episode except in the final, suspense-filled segment when someone almost dies, someone almost overhears a private conversation, or someone is almost kissed.

On this particular summer day, JoEllen and I are taking our leisure in the front yard where we are taking turns swinging or being pushed in the swing Daddy has hung for us from the high limb of the front-yard oak. June bugs are still whizzing about, providing a bit of rural music, but mostly it is quiet—and hot! Oh my, is it hot! We have not had even a hint of a shower for several weeks, so the road between our house and the pasture is ankle-deep in dust. Then we hear it: a low rumble, a chug, a sharp noise when the blade hits a heavy rock in the road. It's the road scrape! We jump from the swing and run down the road towards Mr. Tatum's house to try to get a glimpse of the big machine coming our way. All we can see is a huge cloud of dust as the road scrape makes its way to us. Excitedly, we race back up to the house to tell Mother and Daddy it's coming.

"Well, now," Daddy allows. "That's good news 'cause every time the County sends out the road scrape, I can count on it raining! Yes sir, that's good news!"

Mother is just the opposite in her reaction.

"Oh, Lordy, no! Just what I need – more dust!" she moans as she sets the iron upright and gazes out the window. "Hurry up and help me pull these windows down before it gets here. I don't want all that red dust covering up everything in the house!'

We grab the sticks that hold up the windows in the living room and dining room and let the lower sashes down carefully while Mother gets the ones we can't reach over the stove and sink in the kitchen. She even slams the back door although we don't think the dust will come all the way around the house. As soon as we let down the windows in the bedrooms, we tear outside again to wait for the scraper to come by. It is the largest piece of equipment we have ever seen, mustard yellow with an eight-foot blade between its two axles. The driver sits high up in the cab located over the rear axle and guides the blade along one side of the dirt road so that it smooths out the holes, tire gullies, and large rocks, leaving a pile of dust and dirt in the middle of the road. The scrape will remove this dirt on the return trip when the other side of the road is scraped.

It makes an awful racket that thrills and scares us at the same time. We cower on the porch until it passes the lower drive-way, then tumble across the yard and into the road to see what treasures the blade has turned up. Sometimes we find colored glass or old cans, but mostly we discover rocks of all shapes and sizes. Some are broken where the blade has hit them just right, and some are rounded from many years of lying under the packed red dirt. We gather up all we can carry and haul our stash to the side yard where we store it for later use as the outline of a playhouse we will carve out in the dirt driveway. Then we scurry back to the porch to await the return trip of the road scrape to smooth out the other side of the road. We watch in awe as it passes by, the red dust filling our nostrils and even making us cough a little. That's okay with us because we soon hear the big plow coming that follows the road scrape and "pulls the ditches." Off we go to the middle of the yard to get a closer look at this much smaller and less noisy machine as it slowly makes its way past our house, clearing the ditches and leaving little mounds of red dirt on each side of the road, sort of like a dirt curb. Unlike our mother, we clearly love the day the road scrape comes up our road and breaks the monotony of a summer day. Not much can beat it, except perhaps the Rolling Store.

When we lived in White, the Rolling Store came by our house two or three times a year. I am sure that Mr. and Mrs. Daniel, who owned the general merchandise store across the road from our house, were less than thrilled to see this contraption coming, but JoEllen and I thought it was quite a wonder. It is difficult to describe just what it looked like. The best I can do is to say it was a wooden, rectangular box built around an old, flatbed truck and extending over the cab so that the front end of the truck was barely visible. It looked like a huge box on wheels with no driver, but of course there was one. It had two rear doors that the driver opened when he made a business stop. Just inside the doors, he kept a small set of steps that he put down so that customers could climb up and into the "store" and peruse his goods. He had stick candy, pots and pans, several bolts of fabric, nails and bolts in barrels attached to the side walls with metal straps, molasses, various salves and ointments, and all sorts of other items to interest rural families. I cannot recall ever actually buying anything from the Rolling Store, mainly because Mother refused to allow us to enter such an outlandish vehicle if she got to us before Daddy lifted us into the back. He thought it was a good experience, but Mother thought it was practically sinful. Perhaps the Rolling Store's owner had girly calendars like the ones rumored to line the walls of the 4-Way Café in Cartersville, or maybe he sold punchboards, a game that Mother considered gambling. Whatever the reason, part of the thrill for us was the notion that we were treading on forbidden property by entering the big wooden box known as the Rolling Store.

When I left home for West Georgia College in the fall of 1963, I gladly traded the dust and red dirt, the noise of road scrapes and rolling stores for asphalt highways and concrete sidewalks and the hum of small-town traffic. Today, John and I live inside the city limits of Carrollton on a paved street with a concrete drive-way. Still, sometimes, especially after a brief summer shower, I get a whiff of the distinct aroma of Southern red dirt, and my mind drifts back to my childhood and the many experiences I shared with my family of four. I can almost hear the road scrape or the Rolling Store rumbling up the road and the excited chatter of little girls as they anticipate something new and different coming around the bend.

Cousins

Big Mama, our maternal grandmother, was always the one to get the word out that everyone on her side of the family was expected to gather for dinner (the noonday meal) on a particular Sunday that she deemed an appropriate family occasion. The gathering place might be at her house or at one of her daughters' houses, at Cross Roads Baptist, or at Bartow Presbyterian in Pine Log. These Sundays came around in celebration of every possible holiday: Christmas, Thanksgiving, and Easter, but also Mother's Day, Valentine's Day, Big Mama's birthday, Homecoming at Crossroads Baptist, and any and all church revivals. **Everyone** meant all her children, their spouses, and all the grandchildren and maybe a close friend or two whom all of us thought of as kin. If the friend was female, we called her Aunt So-and-So; if male, then he was Uncle So-and-So, even though there was no blood relation at all. The only kinfolks possibly excused from these gatherings were Aunt Edythe (our real aunt) and her family since they lived all the way down in Macon until around 1954 and then clear over in Forest Park, Georgia, where both Aunt Edythe and her husband Uncle Frank were employed by S and S cafeteria with Sundays being their busiest days. Uncle Nathan (our real uncle) and his family were also excused some of the time because they, too, lived far away, first in Smyrna and later in Social Circle. The rest of us lived in Bartow County and were expected to show up right after church. That meant good food and lots of playtime for the Lipscomb cousins, except JoEllen who claims that she ALWAYS had to wash the dishes. There were sixteen of us grandchildren altogether: Wesley, Judy, Jackie, JoEllen, Anne, Lint, Brenda Gail, Beth, Joey, Stanley, Veda, Linda, Steve, Gary, Melody and Holly.

Wesley and JoEllen are the oldest. At our Lipscomb family gatherings they usually sat and talked with the grown-ups (after Jo finished washing dishes) until they got tired of hearing the same stories. Then, they just talked to each other. Veda, Gary, and Holly are the youngest "regulars" and stayed with their mamas while the rest of us played. Judy and Jackie are Aunt Edythe's girls and rarely attended, but we were always excited when they did because Judy is close to the same age as Linda and I. Joey and Beth belong to Uncle Nathan and came to these gatherings about three times a year. Sometimes, Steve, Stanley, and Melody were included in the play of the Fearsome Foursome: Linda, Lint, Brenda Gail, and Anne. Brenda Gail was much too young for us at the time, but she cried and told on us if we didn't let her play, so she got to tag along on many of our adventures. And what adventures we had!

Every May we all met for the Mother's Day gathering held at Bartow Cumberland Presbyterian. As soon as the meal was over, the four of us (and anyone else close to us in age) headed to the woods to look for maypops and "jugs," the sweet smelling bloom of a forest shrub. We stomped the maypops to see who could make the most noise and saved the "jugs" for our mothers who probably threw them away the first chance they got because the aroma is extremely strong, almost sickening, especially after an afternoon in a warm, closed car. While in the woods, we were always on the look-out for snakes, but we rarely saw one. I suppose the notion that snakes are more scared of us than we are of them is true. Once, however, we did come upon a real monster of a snake. It was dark brown with several raised grayish-looking hackles on its back. Our screams of terror filled the air and brought our fathers running. Our "snake" turned out to be a pine tree limb that had fallen in the leaves and grown a bit of fungus on itself. Because we didn't bother to get a good look at the snake before raising our shouts, we had to go inside the church for the rest of the afternoon service – mostly four-part harmony singing with a bit of preaching thrown in for good measure. Most of the cousins put their heads in their mother's laps and took a nap, but the Fearless Foursome giggled and squirmed enough that we finally had to be separated. I know of at least two of us who were threatened with a switching if we didn't "sit up straight and act like we had good sense."

In the 1950's when we were growing up, it was not unusual for Linda, Brenda Gail, and me to gang up on Lint. At one Big Mama affair, probably Palm Sunday since that particular gathering was usually at our house, I decided to take the four of us on a little hike to see the spring on the back side of our property. Although it was only about a 10-minute walk over a small rise and through some woods, the three others had no idea where we were heading. In a moment of sheer meanness, I whispered to Linda and Brenda Gail that Lint should be left behind. "After all, he is a boy and doesn't really belong with us," I said. For some reason, they agreed, and while Lint was distracted by the spring, we slipped away and ran home. Not long afterwards, one of the grown-ups noticed that Lint was missing, and of course, Miss Brenda Gail tattled. Mother made me get a switch from the hedge and really blistered my and Linda's legs while Daddy went to get poor Lint. Of course, Brenda Gail got off scot-free because she was so young.

Another time but still at our house, Brenda Gail, Linda, and I (don't know where Lint was at the time) got into a bit of a mess down in the front pasture. We should have known better since we all lived on farms, but neither our logic nor our rural upbringing came into play that particular afternoon. We were giggling and having a big time when Linda noticed that three of Daddy's big old Poland China hogs were heading our way.

"Quick!" she hollered. "Climb up in this tree. My daddy says pigs are mean and will eat us up if we stay here!" She was quite convincing (or we were just gullible), so into the nearby apple tree we went. And sure enough, the pigs came after us – or so we thought. We yelled for Daddy, but he couldn't hear us over the roar of the tractor, so we threw apples at the pigs. Naturally, the pigs loved the unexpected treats and stayed right where they were as we pounded them with delicious fruit. The pigs finally became bored – or full of apples -- and ambled away. At last we were free to carefully climb down, exhausted by our "near-death" experience.

Still another adventure occurred without me or Lint but included Judy who was spending the week with Linda. Brenda Gail was also spending the night with Linda when the three of them decided they really needed a Co-Cola. Since there were none in the house, their only recourse was to take Uncle Harry's black station wagon and make the short trip to the store. Oh, I forgot to mention that it was after midnight, and the girls had on their shorty pajamas with their hair in rollers. Also, Linda was 15, Judy 13, and Brenda Gail was barely 12, so no one had a license to drive. Linda was under the wheel and had the empty bottles near her feet to return for deposit when they picked up the new Cokes. These empty bottles prevented her from hitting the dimmer switch when they met another car on the road.

They will not say that they were speeding, but either their speed or their lack of dim lights caused a local deputy to pull them over. Noting their age and obvious nervousness, he became quite concerned that they might be run-aways. Fortunately, Linda piped up that she was Harry Lipscomb's daughter and lived just up the road. The deputy happened to know Uncle Harry and Aunt Sara Nell and let them go with a warning, but they learned a lesson they have never forgotten: they always get dressed and brush their hair (and maybe even put on lipstick) before going out for a Coke after midnight.

There are now just thirteen of the original sixteen Lipscomb cousins. Joey (son of Nathan and Sara) died in 2008, and Jackie (daughter of Edythe and Frank) passed away in 2018. In 2020, we lost Stanley, son of Will and Vera. We have also lost two cousins-in-law: Steve's wife Robyn in 2017, and Veda's husband James in 2020. Joey's sister Beth and her husband live up in Cumming, Georgia, so we see them only on special occasions. Holly, her husband, and their family live in Arizona, so we rarely have a chance to be with them. Steve is the Very Reverend Steve Lipscomb (Really? Steve?), former Dean of the Episcopal Cathedral in Topeka, Kansas. We don't get see him or his son Ian and his family very often. We were all heart-broken for him when he lost his sweet wife Robyn to cancer, but God has smiled on him once more, and his lovely wife Christine joined the family in 2019. As noted earlier, Linda resides in California. Fortunately, she flies home regularly, so I get to visit with her about every five or six months. She and husband Pete have two sons, Ryan and Patrick, and a daughter Blaine. The rest of us -- Wesley, Judy, Melody, Gary, Veda, Brenda Gail, Lint, JoEllen and I -- all live within a 100 mile radius of each other, and most of us are on hand when there is a very important gathering at Wofford's Cross Roads Baptist or when there is a death in the family. In fact, JoEllen, Brenda Gail, and I have become known as the "funeral brigade" because the three of us attend distant funerals together, sometimes staying a night or two on the road. Veda and Wesley are still active members at Cross Roads, so they see each other all the time. Linda, Brenda Gail, and I also stay in close contact. Along with our spouses, the six of us spent a week together in 2012 at Linda and Pete's family cabin in Wisconsin and whiled away most of our time telling lies about our childhood. John and I visited Linda and Pete when they lived in England, again when they moved to New York, and several times during the past three decades that they have resided in California. John and I joined Brenda Gail and Henry for bareboat sailing in the BVI's in 2006 (one of our all-time favorite vacations), and then Linda and Pete joined the Tysons for a similar trip in 2009.

    When Linda is in Georgia, Brenda Gail and I make sure we all get together. Sometimes we even let Lint or JoEllen join in. And when we visit, we always giggle and retell stories of our past adventures, especially those we enjoyed together at one of Big Mama's gatherings. There is just nothing in the whole wide world quite like sharing family history!

First 9 of the 16 Lipscomb Cousins

Front: Brenda Gail and Steve

Middle: Lint, Stanley, and Wesley

Back: JoEllen, Anne, Linda, and Judy

Five of the 14 Bell Cousins

L to R: Opal, Nancy, JoEllen, Kat, and Syble

I wrote the poem on the following page shortly after returning from our sailing adventure in the BVI's with Brenda Gail and Henry.

Sailor's Song

I've not traveled far, nor set the wind free,
But I've stood at mid-ships on an azure sea.
My eyes have not seen all they yearn to take in,
But I've seen a sail furl when it catches the wind.

I've not tasted the whole that my tongue could desire,
But I've sampled sweet lobster from a sandy beach fire.
I've not heard the total that my ears long to hear,
But I've heard the surf crashing --thunderous and clear.

I've not tramped the soil of far-away lands,
But I've felt riggings burn as they slipped through my hands.
From starboard to port, from the bow to the stern,
I've walked the wet decking and watched the winds turn.

I've tasted the salt of the fresh ocean tide.
I've heard the gulls calling, their vessel the sky.
I've felt the wheel tug; I've heard the keel sigh.
I've battled the rain and set the sails high.

I've slept under stars in a black canopied night,
Rocked softly to sleep in the gossamer light.
I've set my face westward away from the shore.
I've hoisted the sails and pulled on the oar.

I've not traveled far, nor sat among kings;
I've heard few of the strains of a violin's strings
But I've danced to the timbre in God's symphony
Among seagulls and dolphins in a cerulean sea.

I've napped in the sunlight, clung to the mast.
I've befriended the future, caught a glimpse of the past.
I've heard the great mourning of a ship under sail,
I've visited the reef; I've sounded the bell.

I've not traveled far, not set the wind free;
I've written no songs, no sweet melodies.
But I've anchored my boat, I've sailed wind and lee,
And my soul overflows with its song of the sea

Opposites Really Do Attract

My parents were quite a couple. Pictures of their young years before JoEllen and I came along reveal a tall, attractive young woman with curly black hair, pretty brown eyes, and a sweet smile. The young man by her side has a broad grin and is wearing a natty outfit with a hat cocked to one side. They appear to be quite happy and enjoying their life together. During all my growing up years, I do not remember ever hearing them argue for more than a few minutes, yet I always knew that they were very different kinds of people.

Mother (Sally Jo Lipscomb Bell) was the youngest of three daughters born to Mary Nida Collins and Joseph Linton Lipscomb. All four of her brothers, Nathan, Harry, Will Henry, and Walt, were younger. Even with six siblings, I have the impression that Mother felt as if she grew up alone. Her sisters, Edythe and Ruth, were only fifteen months apart and were very close. Their mother held Edythe at home until Ruth was old enough to start to school so that the two of them went all through school together. Mother was two years behind them, and her nearest brother, Nathan, was two years behind her, so she was in a grade by herself.

After finishing tenth grade, Mother's parents sent her to live with her uncle and aunt in Calhoun, Bob and Mildred Collins. There, she finished high school and acted as nanny for Uncle Bob and Aunt Mildred's three children, Pat, Robin, and Ted. When she talked of her time in Calhoun, it was clear to me that she loved living there and making new friends even though she worked very hard to keep up her grades, play first-string guard on the Calhoun High basketball team, and keep the children after school and at night when her uncle and aunt went out. She was very disappointed when her parents brought her back to their house the summer after she graduated. She once told me that the only reason they brought her home was to have one more hand to work in the field.

When Mother and Daddy married, they truly did not have "a pot to pee in." However, Mother did her best to give their life together some beauty. She was an excellent seamstress and made all her clothes, and later, all the clothes that JoEllen and I wore, including our panties and slips. She made Daddy's shirts and underwear for years and even made sheets for our beds. She covered open shelves with homemade drapes made from flour sacks (the fabric she used for everything else) and sewed cushions for chairs and curtains for the windows. She loved her flowers and grew some of the most beautiful dahlias and hydrangeas in the area. She once planted hollyhocks at the end of the house. These flowers grew so tall we could see the blooms at the top of the kitchen windows five feet off the ground!

Mother was always busy with housework, canning and freezing, or working in the field alongside our father. There was little time for social calls. I don't remember that anyone came to visit other than her sister Ruth, Daddy's sister Corene, or other family members, but I am convinced she longed for a close friend. I know she got really excited when it was her turn to have the Women's Missionary Society meeting at our house. She would write out her plan for refreshments and spend hours cleaning and scrubbing the house before the ladies came. If the meeting fell during the summer months, she usually served her delicious chicken salad on a lettuce leaf with pimento cheese finger sandwiches (no crust), sliced tomatoes, and iced tea. For dessert, she usually prepared a fresh coconut cake. I vividly remember watching her use a hammer and nail to bleed the milk from the coconut and then crack it open with the hammer and scrape out the white stuff inside to grate for the cake. If the meeting happened to fall during an autumn or winter month, she always served German chocolate cake and hot Russian tea. Both had a wonderful aroma that filled the house all afternoon.

Mother taught the Junior Sunday School class at Woffords's Cross Roads Baptist for forty-two years. She knew her Bible better than anyone I know. On Sundays when the pastor announced his text, she could turn right to it without thinking. She knew many, many verses by heart but never flaunted her knowledge. She prayed beautiful prayers and sang about her faith at home as well as from the pulpit at church as a soloist. She participated in as many charitable projects as she could manage, often serving as chairperson and working long into the night making notes and gathering information so that she was always prepared when a group met to discuss a particular subject or to plan an activity.

Working outside the home was always in the back of Mother's mind. She once worked as a census taker, a job that nearly did her in. It meant long, long hours and lots of paperwork, but she followed it through to the end, mainly because we were pretty desperate for income. A year or so later, she went to work part-time at Munn's Stationery Shop in Cartersville as a bookkeeper. Again, she worked above and beyond what others would have done in her place with very little acknowledgement from her employer. Eventually, the shop no longer needed her, and she was home again. When Ray Kown, a member of our church, needed a bookkeeper, she went to work for him and really enjoyed her position, but the job she wanted most was to be the Postmistress of the White Post Office. She studied and studied before taking the Civil Service exam that was required for eligibility. Her score was higher than the one earned by the man who was also interested in the job, but he was hired because he got extra points for being a veteran. In addition to her job as Ray's bookkeeper, Mother became the part-time postal clerk. She took her job very seriously, but she never quite got over losing the higher postal position she really wanted.

Whenever JoEllen or I needed help with schoolwork, Mother was always there to give us clues and encouragement. She never doubted that we would both graduate high school with honors and go on to college. She made our cheerleading uniforms and helped us learn our cheers. She attended all the home games, even going to football games, a sport she knew very little about and did not enjoy watching. I hope she was able to relive some of her cherished memories of Calhoun High School basketball when she sat in the stands at Cass to watch us cheer for the Colonels.

Mother was a very strict disciplinarian, one we dared not disappoint, but we always knew she loved us. She kept a hickory switch on top of the refrigerator but rarely used it. Most of the time, she controlled us with a look that kept us in our place. Having a mother who believed in us and set the example of kindness and good works has certainly molded us into the women we have become.

When Mother was in her late seventies, JoEllen and I began to notice that she was becoming forgetful and that little things that should not be a bother agitated her more than a little bit. At the time, she was caring for Daddy who had had several strokes, so we attributed her problems to exhaustion and tried to alleviate some of her stress by visiting more often and doing some of her chores for her. After Daddy's death, she stabilized a bit, and together, the three of us negotiated the sale of her house to John and Debra Mosher, a couple who had befriended Mother and Daddy and had asked long before Daddy died about purchasing their property. As part of the deal, we reserved one-half acre just below the old house where we constructed a new house for Mother. She had always dreamed of building a home, so the time spent on plans and the actual construction kept her busy and relatively happy. With a few adjustments, the house Mother originally drew on the back of an envelope turned out to be just right for her. It had two bedrooms, two and a half baths, a large eat-in kitchen, a living room/dining room combination, and a small den on the back. Beside the den was a tiny laundry/freezer room, and she had a good sized front porch. She was really proud to finally have a brand new house, but often wished aloud that Daddy could have enjoyed it with her.

About eighteen months after moving into the new house, Mother's forgetfulness exacerbated. We tried several ways to keep her at home. JoEllen got a Reinhardt student to move in so that Mother would not be alone at night, but Mother often locked the young woman out of the house and eventually got to the point that she didn't know who was staying in the front bedroom. We also had meals delivered to her house, first by a woman who had a small restaurant in White, and then we found Geneva, a lady in

Mother's church who agreed to cook a noonday meal, deliver it to Mother's house, and stay and visit with her for an hour or so every day. Geneva told us later that Mother was surprised to see her every day and never remembered that she had been there just 24 hours earlier. This arrangement worked for a while, but then that too was not enough to sustain Mother's situation. Next, we hired a nurse to move into the house. Her name was Benae, and at first she was wonderful. She still worked as a visiting nurse, but was not gone for more than a few hours a day. She took Mother shopping in Cartersville; they occasionally went to the movies, walked a mile or so each day, and generally had a good time. But as often happens, Mother's mental state deteriorated, and Nurse Benae got less and less attentive. Eventually, we had to do that which no one wants: we moved Mother to the Waldrop Assisted Living Center. Unfortunately, she was too mentally deficient to stay very long, and the process of moving from place to place began. It ended at Pine Knoll Nursing Home in Carrollton after a few weeks in Rome and eight months in a personal care home in Temple. Mother was diagnosed with severe dementia, probably Alzheimer's disease, and did not know JoEllen or me for more than a year before her death on April 19, 2004. She was 87. More than three hundred people paid their respects to her at Owen Funeral Home in Cartersville, and Cross Roads Baptist Church was filled to capacity the next day, a tribute to the wonderful woman she was.

Now Daddy loved Mother dearly and would do almost anything to make her happy, but in truth, they had very different personalities. He petted JoEllen and me nearly to death. He was so afraid we would hurt ourselves that he sometimes kept us from just playing like ordinary kids. He could not supply us with much that involved financial resources, but we definitely reaped the wealth of his love. He read us stories from Little Golden Books (which he pretty much made up since his reading skills were limited to second-grade level), took us with him almost everywhere he went, and taught us right from wrong by example.

Throughout his entire life, Daddy held only one job that did not involve farming; he was a school bus driver for more than 20 years. While he sometimes got very aggravated with the children who acted up on his bus, he also showed his true colors on cold rainy days. Some of the little ones who rode his bus lived "a good ways" off the road. On more than one occasion, he stopped his bus, got off, walked to the house, picked the children up in his arms, and carried them to the bus so they wouldn't get their feet wet.

I imagine that he carried JoEllen almost everywhere the family went before I was born, and I know he carried me until I was much too old and too heavy for such things. On Sunday nights after church, JoEllen and I would both pretend that we were asleep when we arrived home (three whole miles) so that Daddy would carry us inside. And he always did.

Daddy told us that he went "all the way to Thanksgiving break of his second grade year" in school. Then he had to quit to help on the family farm. He was just seven years old and worked all day the same as grown men. He had an older sister (Elma), an older brother (Dick), his twin Corene, and two younger brothers (F.M. and Robert). His parents, Fred Moten and Mary Lena Goss Bell, lived in White near the house we lived in until I was seven. Corene lived with the parents and worked at EZ Mills. Every day after work, Miss Maxie (one of Corene's friends and co-workers) would drop her off at our house, and she would take JoEllen and me home with her so that Mother could go to the barn to milk. Though she was his twin, she looked nothing like Daddy. He was a trim 5' 8," had black hair, brown eyes, and relatively dark skin; Corene was a short, round, blue-eyed, blonde-haired, fair-skinned woman. Daddy was as steady as the day is long, a good driver, and an extremely hard worker; his sister was hair-brained, couldn't drive worth a lick, and was forever dreaming up new ways to get rich quick, which she never did. In fact, the rare arguments that Daddy and Mother had usually stemmed from his bailing out Corene or Dick or F.M. from one or another of their financial misadventures.

Daddy was a deacon at Cross Roads Baptist for well over 50 years, serving as chairman more than a few times. He grew up in the Methodist church but was baptized in the creek near Cross Roads when JoEllen and I were really young. He loved his church and was there practically every time the doors opened. Sometimes he led the Sunday singing when Bill Bishop was absent. He had a really pretty tenor voice and could harmonize on most hymns even though he could not read music. During Bible school, he would rise earlier than usual to get as much done on the farm as he possibly could before time to go to the church to help with the boys' craft time. There is no telling how many arks and crosses he built during those years. He was always ready to participate in Prayer Meeting on Wednesday nights and knew a lot about the Bible. I believe most of his knowledge came from listening carefully to sermons and Sunday School lessons because he could barely read. When he did study his Bible, we could hear him whispering the words aloud as he slowly plowed through chapter and verse.

    Daddy did not have much leisure time, but when he and mother bought a television set, he loved watching several shows. One of his favorites was "Gunsmoke" with Marshall Matt Dillon, Miss Kitty, Chester, and Festus. In later years, he kept up with the time and would actually quit work before dark to come inside to see this western show. However, his all-time favorite was "Live Atlanta Wrestling." He got extremely excited when his man was down (usually one of the Guthrie brothers), and somebody like Freddy Blassie (a bad guy) was cheating by throwing the good guy into the turn-buckle of the ring or calling in his tag-team partner without leaving the ring himself. Daddy would huff and puff, blow out his cheeks, turn red, and holler at the wrestlers and referees until the match was called or somebody won, sitting on the edge of his chair and throwing air punches all the time. When it was over, he would be worn out but would continue to declare that Old So-and-So was cheating!

Always an active man, Daddy did not allow his Myasthenia Gravis (a disease in which the eyelids droop, and it is difficult to swallow) to get him down. A year or so after being diagnosed with MG, he had the first of several strokes. Still, he kept going. He faithfully did his therapy every day and continued to hobble around on a walker until the last few days of his life. He was always cheerful in spite of the hardship, and on his last visit to the hospital, he told me after a particularly difficult session on the breathing machine that he was ready to go home. I talked to the nurses who insisted that the doctor would not allow his dismissal. Still, Daddy was adamant about wanting to leave the hospital, so I did as he said (just the way he taught me). Mother and I gathered up his things, got him in a wheelchair, and left the hospital without the doctor's permission. Wesley, mother's nephew, picked up the hospital bed that belongs to the church and had it set up in the living room when we got home. That night, Jo-Ellen and I sat up and talked all night long, sending Mother to bed to rest after the ordeal of staying in the hospital with Daddy for more than a week. During the night, Daddy occasionally lifted his head and looked at us as if to say, "What are y'all giggling about?" When we asked if he needed anything, he would relax and put his head down but never said a word.

The next morning, August 16, 1997, we greeted the nurse we had contracted with to move in the house to assist Mother through Daddy's final days. The nurse got settled in, made friends with Daddy who was alert but not talking, and JoEllen and I left. When I opened the door at my own home after the one and a half hour drive, the telephone was ringing. Daddy was gone. He was 88. His funeral, held in his beloved church two days later, could not begin to hold all those who came to show their sorrow and respect.

I have tried to convey to others the differences between my parents and have used this example that I think says it all.

If I found myself alone in Timbuktu without family, friends, or a means of financial support, I would borrow a phone and call my parents. If Mother answered, she would say, "Now, Anne, I know how smart you are, and I have all the faith in the world that you will consider how you got yourself into this fix. Then I know you will figure out how to get yourself out the same way. I will be looking forward to seeing you real soon." If Daddy answered the phone, he would say, "Well, hon, you want me to send you the money to get home, or do you want me to come and get you?"

Yes, opposites really do attract!

Sally Jo and Emmett Bell, 1937

**Sally Jo and Emmett Bell
Golden Wedding Anniversary, 1987**

To Daddy

NOTE: *JoEllen wrote the following tribute to Daddy the night of his death, and the minister read it at Daddy's funeral. She knew him well.*

To Daddy

Farmers pray for sons. But if Daddy was disappointed with his two daughters, we never knew it. We always thought we were the apples of his eye.

When we were little girls, he read our "Little Golden books every night . . . over and over . . . as many times as we wanted to hear as we sat on the front porch in the summer at our home in White.

If we were ever sick, we could tell the he wished HE were the sick one. He would beg us to "take this little aspirin (diluted in Coca Cola) with a promise that "as soon as you're well, we'll get those little bedroom shoes with the bunnies on the toe." And he didn't forget.

Every day we got a nickel to spend at Mr. Daniel's store. Now, we know there were many times (way back then) that two nickels were a nuisance to always have on hand -- or a burden to his pocketbook. But he didn't forget.

He carried Anne in his arms until her feet dragged the ground -- and with each step he took, there was JoEllen asking a million questions: "Daddy, why do cows have to be milked?" "Daddy, why do roosters crow but hens cluck?" "Daddy, can we go to town with you on Saturday?" And he answered all the questions, with patience and good humor.

He spanked -- one time -- and it hurt him so much he never spanked again. But his discipline -- thumping us behind the ear and giving us THAT LOOK -- was scarier than any hickory switch.

As we grew older, we could always count on Daddy when we needed someone to teach us arithmetic or to drive the old pick-up; to take us to ballgames; to wait for the school bus to get back from far-away games; to give us the confidence we needed as we became women.

What will we remember most about Daddy? His generosity? His laugh? His kindness? Yes, all these, but mostly we will remember these two things.

First, his HANDS. They were rough and calloused from such hard work (maybe sons could have eased the soreness), but they were tender and caring for two little girls.

And then in later years, his COURAGE. After his stroke, he learned to use his left hand, and it must have been quite a frustrating task, but he never complained. Then in the last few years, when he was very sick, that same courage allowed us the comfort of asking, "Daddy, how are you?" "Oh, porely, porely ... " and then a mischievous smile to let us know he was OK, even if he wasn't.

Daddy, rest now. You gave us so much and asked nothing. For all these things, and so many more, we won't forget you.

Is Convenience Worth the Cost?

Despite the convenience of silk flowers and artificial Christmas trees, Egg-O waffles and microwave popcorn, a fair amount of family connection time may have been lost over the past couple of decades with the introduction of many items that have become commonplace and almost indispensable.

One example is the artificial Christmas tree with its glittering, already-attached mini lights. I readily admit to loving the idea of a tree going up in a couple of hours with no untangling of light strings and no needles to vacuum when the holiday is over. However, I do occasionally wax nostalgic when I pause long enough to think about the hunt for the "perfect" tree that used to accompany the season.

...

"Daddy, when can we go look for a Christmas tree?" I ask as my father is trying to repair some broken fence line.

"I've already got one spotted over in the back pasture," he responds without even looking up from his work.

"Daddy, Joelene and them already have their tree up in the living room; it looks so pretty, all sparkly with its colored lights. Do you think we can go get our tree today?" I beg, trying not to whine because I know whining is not allowed in our family.

"Anne, go see if your mama needs some help in the house. I am busy right now, and you are just aggravating me with your questions! And watch yourself as you cross the road. Now skedaddle! Some folks around here have work to do!"

I burst into tears -- Daddy is mad at me! I run to the house but don't let Mother see that I have cried a little. She does not suffer fools gladly. As I putter about, feeling like I want to *really* cry over not having a tree yet, JoEllen pops her head out of her book and asks, "What's wrong with you?"

"Daddy is too busy with his old fence to take time to go hunt a Christmas tree," I moan.

"Oh! A tree! Yes, that's what we need to do today! Did you ask him if we could go today?" she asks, and with that, JoEllen is up and running to the kitchen to find Mother.

"Mother, Mother! We have to get a Christmas tree today," she shouts as her black and white saddle oxfords slide into the kitchen almost before she does. "Mother, don't you think we need to go find a tree, maybe now?" I am right behind her, adding my "Mother, can we, can we go today?"

Our mother is never idle, and this day is no different from any of the others. She is baking for the big day -- a German chocolate cake with gooey icing that must be cooked to just the right temperature and spread on the cake at just the right time, and she does not need any distractions like a couple of little girls yipping about a Christmas tree.

"What in the world are you two talking about? Can't you see I am in the middle of this cake and that this blasted icing is not working like it's supposed to?" she almost yells -- almost, but not quite. Mother doesn't yell, but she can give us a look that sets us straight in a New York minute. And she gives it to us now. We mumble our apologies and hurry back into the living room to strategize.

"I bet Mother is thinking about a tree right now," I say.

"Yeah, you're right. I bet she wants one today, too. As soon as Daddy comes in to eat, she'll probably suggest we go look for one before he goes back to the pasture," JoEllen says.

"Probably," I say, but not with a whole lot of confidence. We both know that the tree will be cut and two pieces of 2 X 4 will be nailed to the bottom of the trunk in an X shape whenever Daddy can make time. We also know that our tree will not be as tall as we hope for or as rounded or as thick or even as green as most of the trees in the homes of our family and friends. Daddy is notorious for choosing a unique Christmas tree.

When noon finally comes and Daddy whistles his way into the house, we are excited that he seems to be over his frustration with me and is now in a good mood.

"Howdy, Miss Jo," he says to our mother. We perk up immediately. "Miss Jo" is his favorite nickname for her. Mother barely glances his way, but we know she is smiling because her response is low and musical.

"Did you wipe your feet, Hon? Dinner will be on the table in a minute. Go ahead and wash your face and hands. I'll be there directly," she says, and then to our immense and wide-eyed delight, she adds, "I was thinking a while ago about going ahead and getting a Christmas tree pretty soon. What do you think?"

Daddy looks at the two of us huddled together against his knees, and says, "Well, now, I don't suppose old Santy Clause will stop by here if we don't have a lit-up tree in the window. I think I saw just the right one last week over near the three-acre field. I'll take another look in a day or two," he says and gives us a wink.

We are beside ourselves. A Christmas tree! Immediately, we begin to talk about the lights and the ornaments and, our favorite thing, the silver aluminum icicles that Mother saves between two sheets of wax paper from year to year.

"Can we get everything out of the smokehouse right now?" we beg.

"Oh, for goodness sakes! Sit down and eat your dinner, and maybe we will take a look later on this afternoon," Mother says as she gives Daddy her best smile.

We gobble our green beans, mashed potatoes, and cornbread, and swallow the contents of our milk glasses as quickly as possible, babbling on about Christmas and Santa Claus and what we hope he will bring. But mostly, we talk about the tree.

"What does it look like, Daddy?"

"Can we go with you to cut it down?"

"Can I cut it down with the saw, Daddy? I know how already because I have watched you do it for years and years," exclaims JoEllen.

"Is it bigger than the one we had last year? I bet it will reach the ceiling!" I add.

When we finish our meal and Daddy is heading back to the field, we grab our jackets and bounce along behind him, excited as can be. He cautions us along the way to watch out for this dip in the path so that we don't fall and to be careful of those briars that will scratch our arms. He holds two strands of barbed wire apart for us to crawl through when we get to the cross fence. At last, he arrives at the spot he is working on and lets us hand him nails and the hammer even though he could do it himself in half the time. We pepper him with questions about the location of the tree and ask him what time he thinks he will be finished about a dozen times even though we know he will not take the time to reach inside his overall pocket to look at his pocket watch, and I can't tell time yet anyway.

At last, he raises up, stretches his back and says, "Guess we better get on to the house."

Our faces fall, and our chatter ceases. What about the tree? We have waited all afternoon!

And then our Daddy picks us both up at the same time and heads across the pasture towards the three-acre field. We kick and laugh and generally make a ruckus, but there is no place we had rather be at that moment than in his arms on our way to get a Christmas tree.

The tree he has picked out suits us just fine. It is a cedar tree that has grown up against the fence. Daddy produces a small hacksaw from the back pocket of his overalls and begins to fell the mighty tree. It is about four and a half, maybe five feet tall, but we are not that big, so it looks huge to us. When he gets it down, he hoists it over his shoulder, and off we go to the house.

Mother has gotten the four strings of colored lights out of the boxes and is working on getting them to light by changing first one bulb and then another. Our Aunt Sara Nell has bubble lights for their tree. At the bottom of each light is a small round container and above it is a candle-like spire about three inches tall with a point at the top. When the string is plugged in, little bubbles come up from the bottom, one at a time, and somehow disappear at the point. I love those lights! But our multicolored bulbs look wonderful too. JoEllen and I start to flatten out the icicles while Daddy is outside making a stand out of two pieces of board and nailing them to the tree trunk. When he hauls it inside, Mother starts to laugh and pronounces that he has done it again!

Our tree is very, very lopsided due to its growth against the fence. It also has several dead spots, probably where a cow rubbed up against it to scratch her back. Additionally, the stand is so wobbly that Mother has to fold up some old newspaper to stick under one side to make it sort of stand up straight. The top lists to one side so she will have a really hard time making the aluminum-foil-and-cardboard star stay put. Nevertheless, JoEllen and I are thrilled. We have our Christmas tree at last, and when all the lights (maybe 45 to 50 bulbs in all) are strung around the limbs, and the decorations are hung along with the silvery icicles, we declare it the best tree ever! Nowadays, we would call it a "Charlie Brown" tree, but in the 1950's, it was a showpiece!

The wonderful aroma of a live Christmas tree is almost nonexistent now, and another casualty of modern convenience is the wood cook stove. We got our first electric stove when I was about eleven years old. Until then, our kitchen was always cozy in the wintertime because a fire had to be kept going in the stove to prepare the meals, AND it was always a veritable oven in the summer because we still had to have a fire, even in 90 degree weather, for meal preparation. I spent many hours near that stove with my mother as she made teacakes (which she kept in the warming oven of the stove), canned green beans and tomatoes, or did any other chores that required the use of the stove or the sink. I did my homework on the kitchen table. I listened to Mother's afternoon radio stories with her, also in the kitchen because that is where we kept our one radio, a turquoise affair about 10 inches long and 6 inches high with gold and white knobs for volume and tuning in to the local stations. I watched her cut out dresses for us on the table, and I helped her punch down the dough when she was making yeast rolls. Mother liked to sing, and I learned the lyrics to many, many hymns and popular songs listening to her sing as she worked around the kitchen and kept the fire going in the wood stove. When my own daughter was growing up, she often spent some of her time with me in the kitchen, but with central heat and air conditioning, she usually wandered off after a bit to her own room to do homework or to talk on the phone with friends. Our son is an outdoor guy; when he was growing up, he rarely spent time inside, and when he did, it was usually in his room where he had his trains and cowboys and Indians or in the living room with the televison. I never quite perfected the skill to make teacakes that taste like the ones baked in a wood cook stove, and I preferred to sew by myself without the distraction of a little boy and little girl watching and asking questions. But like Mother, I often sing when I work. Unfortunately, I doubt if my children remember any of the lyrics of my favorite songs, and I know my daughter didn't learn how to cut out dresses by watching me do so on the kitchen table by the warmth of a wood stove. Perhaps the convenience of my gas stove and my own space to sew hindered the opportunity for my children to get to know their mother better. Looking back, that convenience was not worth the cost of time I could have spent with two of my favorite three people in the world. I expect you know the third is their father.

Certainly, there are a number of little things we knew how to do and chores we performed when JoEllen and I were children simply because that is the era in which we grew up. The woodstove provided just one. A daily chore was to bring in the "sto-wood" (stove wood) which Daddy had split and stacked in the back yard. Each piece of wood was about 8 inches long and 2 to 3 inches wide. I would first load JoEllen's extended arms with about 6-7 pieces, so she could carry them inside to the woodbox. Then, she would load me up, and I would make my trip in. Not a big job, but one we had to do each day to keep the family stove going so we could eat. The added bonus was the opportunity to learn how to work together to accomplish a task.

One of our favorite meals in the wintertime was sorghum syrup and hot buttered biscuits fresh out of the cook stove's oven. There is definitely a skill, perhaps even an art, to eating sorghum syrup. First, the jar has to be opened, and that is not always easy because the syrup is so sticky that it becomes gluelike if the rim is not carefully cleaned after each use. Once the jar is coaxed into opening by beating around the edges of the lid with the handle of a table knife and using a dishtowel to get a good grip, the syrup must be precisely poured on to the plate. The skill comes into play when the pourer is ready to stop the flow. The jar is tipped back but not too far as to let the liquid run down the outside of the jar; then, the flow is cut off by scraping a table knife across the rim and through the syrup. Presto! The syrup stops and a pool is left in the plate, ready to be scooped onto the freshly buttered biscuit, also by using a table knife. No spoons or forks necessary for this meal. I know people who stir butter into their syrup, but we preferred to put lots of the creamy yellow stuff on our hot biscuits and follow up with syrup. There is still nothing better on a cold winter night.

JoEllen and I spent a lot of our cold winter afternoons as well as many lazy summer days with Corene, Daddy's old-maid twin sister. We called Corene "Dean," but I do not know why. She lived in White with Granny and Granddad, our paternal grandparents, in a pretty white frame house about 800 yards or so from the old house our father rented from Mr. Yancy. To get there, we could walk across the road in front of our place, pass an old warehouse where chenille rugs were once made, then pass in front of the McKeever's house, and finally turn right into the dirt driveway at Granny and Granddad's. But the best way home was over the foot log of a small creek that ran behind the McKeever's home and the warehouse. Crossing that foot log to Dean's house must have been a major skill because neither of us ever learned how to do it. Instead, Daddy picked us up one at a time and carried us across to make sure we did not fall in. I remember exactly what it looked like. It was about 8 feet long and maybe 7 inches wide, just enough for a man's foot so that he could walk across a stream, one foot in front of the other, without getting his brogans wet. In addition to the narrow width, the log was always slick with watery mold and mildew. It took balance to cross, and to walk it with a squirming child in arms must have been quite a feat, but Daddy had a lot of practice because he carried us across every weekday afternoon until we moved away to Sunrise Valley when I was seven years old.

From Dean, we learned several skills that are, like cook stoves and foot logs, of another time and place. Dean loved to brush and style our hair, especially mine because it was fine and silky, unlike JoEllen's coarse crown of tight curls. When we were old enough to control our small hand movements, she taught us to make pincurls. After shampooing our hair in the kitchen sink, she would pull out a strand of hair about an inch wide, and starting at the end, curl it around her index finger until she reached the scalp, slide it off the tip of her finger against our heads, and slip a bobby pin through it. When our hair got dry, the bobby pins came out, a brush went through, and my hair had beautiful blonde waves all over. JoEllen's? Not so much -- she just went from curly to curlier. When I reached my teens, I started pin-curling my own hair and did so until I was in college and learned to use large pink foam rollers instead of bobby pins.

    Dean also helped us practice our Sword Drill skills by calling out a Scripture chapter and verse and having us quickly turn to it in our Bibles -- little white ones that she gave us when we were in her junior Sunday School class at Cross Roads. I still have mine. She sometimes painted our nails to look like hers and Miss Maxie's. When she didn't forget, she would remove it before Daddy came to get us after he and Mother got finished with the milking. Mother was not a fan of nail polish, especially on 5 and 8 year olds.

    Once we moved into the house on the farm, we learned to milk, drive the tractor, and pitch hay along with other chores required to keep a small farm running. I should say, JoEllen learned to milk. I was no good at it because I was afraid of the cows and because JoEllen preferred milking over washing dishes. There is a true skill when it comes to milking. Mother tried to teach me, and I did do it a time or two when I had to. First, the milker must tie the cow's head to the railing in the barn so she won't back over the milker. Next, the udder has to be washed. Poor cow! In the winter, that water was really cold. Then, the bucket is set under the udder, and the milking begins. The thumb is placed on one of the cow's teats on the side closest to the milker. The index and middle fingers go behind the teat and on the side away from the milker. When set, the thumb is pushed against the teat towards the fingers and pulled down, stripping out the milk, not squeezing it out. My biggest problems were squeezing when I was supposed to be stripping and jumping out of the way of the cow's tail when she squished it at me. Besides, driving the tractor was much more fun than milking, and pitching hay was easy after the first day when our arms were sore from the unfamiliar motion of lifting and throwing the hay onto the haystack or up into the loft of the barn. And the best part came after the pitching -- lying on our backs in a pile of that sweet-smelling pasture hay.

    I suppose all generations have skills and traditions that are peculiar to their own time. Some of those from my younger days are no longer a part of life. Perhaps new skills are just as important and worthwhile, but old ones like choosing the perfect Christmas tree from the pasture, walking the foot log, and milking by hand constitute some of my very best memories of when we lived in the big old house in White and later on a little farm with a view of the timeless Blue Ridge mountains -- just the four of us.

In the Corners of My Mind

Sometimes when I am out and about, I get a glimpse of someone, just for a fraction of a second, who looks exactly like Mother or Daddy, even though both of them have been gone for many years. Other times, a song or a sermon or a conversation with friends will remind me of a time long passed. Most of these flashes of memory last for only a moment and then fade into the corners of my mind. Even though these fragments are not full-length stories, I am including a few bits and pieces of years long ago so that the "evidence of things hoped for and the substance of things not seen" will not be lost.

*****JoEllen and I always got new dresses and new shoes for Easter. Until we were ten or so, the shoes were black patent Mary Janes. We kept them shiny by rubbing them with a half biscuit or a bit of Vaseline every Saturday night. The oil in the biscuit/Vaseline did wonders for scuffed shoes. The dresses were almost always organdy or dotted Swiss with full gathered skirts and a large sash that tied in a big bow in the back. When I was under five, the dresses included a matching pinafore that went over the dress, all hand-made by our mother. I have looked and looked, but sadly, I don't have any pictures of Jo-Ellen and me in our Easter finery. We also got a new outfit to wear the last Sunday of Pine Log Camp Meeting. Once, Mother bought us navy dusters -- dress length, light weight coats made of file material with three-quarter push-up sleeves. I loved that duster and wore mine for a couple of years and then wore JoEllen's two or three more years when she got too tall for it. This little coat was one hand-me-down that I loved getting. The only other time we got new clothes was at the beginning of each school year. I always looked forward to fall and new shoes, except one time when we both got clunky, oxblood, lace-up oxfords. They were the ugliest shoes ever made and would not wear out no matter how many times we tried to bang them up and get them wet. I don't know why our parents bought those particular shoes; maybe they were all they could afford at the time. I do know that both of us hated them and were delighted when Easter finally came, and we got new Mary Janes. In the fall, those awful shoes had thankfully disappeared. I think Mother hated them as much as we did. My all-time favorite shoes were the low-cut, black and white saddle oxfords with a tiny buckle on the back that I had to have for my cheerleading uniform when I was in ninth grade. A box-pleated, above-the-knee navy skirt, a white buttoned-down collar blouse, and a white corduroy vest with four gold buttons on the front and the Cass High logo of a Confederate Colonel on the back made up the rest of the ensemble. We girls really looked spiffy and even had our photograph made wearing these outfits in the Macon newspaper during the championship basketball game in the winter of 1960.

***** The Goatman was a legend in the rural South when I was growing up. We could hear him coming from at least a mile away because his goat-pulled wagon was stacked with pots and pans, old furniture, worn-out tires, license plates, and every other kind of junk imaginable. We could also smell him coming because folks said he never bathed, brushed his teeth, combed his long hair or scraggledy beard, or changed his clothes. Also, his 8-10 goats were his constant companions; they provided him with milk and kept him warm on a cold winter night. I learned from a newspaper article that his name was Charles McCartney and that he made his living by charging a dollar to have his picture made by anyone interested in doing so. However, the only way we knew of him was when we heard someone cry, "The Goatman is coming! The Goatman is coming!"

*****The "Farm to Table" dining experience that has gained in popularity during the past several years is definitely not a new idea. All those who came before us, as far back as history records, have eaten this way. The four of us were no exception: we, too, ate farm to table, but we didn't know that it was the "environmentally friendly, heart-heathy" thing to do. For us, it was the only way to eat since we rarely visited a grocery store or produce market. Our garden provided.

***** We never had a decent car or truck. Most of the time, when we had to go somewhere with Daddy in the truck, we were in good company because many of the other farmers' trucks were in pretty much the same shape as his. But the cars! Oh, we despised being seen in some of those old things. One was a rattle-trap Chevrolet, dark blue on the outside with brown cloth seats inside. It must have been about a '40 or '41 model when we had it in 1957. It was not only old, but rusted in spots and very loud. When we went to town, JoEllen and I found something that needed attending to in the floorboard so that our friends would not see us in that car. Once, we "inherited" Big Mama's dark green Plymouth. It was not much better than the Chevrolet, but at least she had not allowed it to get rusty, and it was not quite as out of date as our other vehicles. It was this car that JoEllen backed into the septic tank that Daddy was digging out in the backyard. Perhaps she did it on purpose in an effort to get rid of it. It didn't work. We kept it for years and years.

I learned to drive when I was 12 in a poor excuse for a truck. I have no idea what model or year it was, but by the time we owned it, its hood had several holes rusted through, the rear end was dented in more than one place, and it was difficult to determine the original color due to the many brown primer coats of paint that were scattered over the body. Like the hood, the floorboard was rusted out. Dust flew up into our faces as we chugged along, but the funniest part of the whole truck was the clutch. It didn't have one. Instead, Daddy had jerry-rigged it with a heavy piece of wire that stretched from somewhere underneath the hood to just below and beside the brake pedal. To change gears, we had to bend down, reach and grab the wire, pull it up and shift quickly so that we could once again look up and out the windshield to see if we were still in the road. It's a good thing that cars and trucks didn't travel at high speeds back then; we would not have survived.

I drove the tractors and trucks around the farm until I was 16, then I got my license. Even this part of my driving experience is a bit unusual. I never took a written test or a driving test. The big day happened to be a rainy one, and Daddy had bargained with a neighbor to buy his hay. It had been baled and was ready to pick up, but that meant either Daddy or I had to drive the truck while the other drove the tractor home on the public road between Pine Log and our barn. Daddy knew the sheriff, so he quickly drove the two of us to Cartersville, told the sheriff about his dilemma, and said I could drive with or without a license, but I was going to drive regardless. The sheriff gave me my license, sans tests, and off we went to the pasture to pick up the hay.

Old cars and old trucks are not in my garage today. I love a new, fancy car -- one that I enjoy being seen in rather than one that calls for hiding in the floorboard. And I am certain I would have to study if I were ever required to take a driving test.

***** Linda and I were mischievous and sometimes got into a little bit of trouble, but we never really did anything terrible. Sometimes, however, we pushed the limits of our mothers' patience, and one of them would feel it necessary to give us a light switching to set us back on the path of goodness. When we lived in the two-story house in White, one of the community projects my parents set for the family was to occasionally clean off the dead flowers on the graves at the cemeteries at Cross Roads as well as those in the White Cemetery near our house. Mother hated to see good ribbons go to waste, so if she came across an arrangement that still had a pretty good-looking ribbon, she brought it home and stored it for later use in one of the rooms upstairs. Now the upstairs was off-limits for children because it had never been finished -- just a set of beautiful old stairs that led up to a hallway and two unfinished rooms. At the landing at the top of the stairs was a door that opened onto a small balcony, definitely not a place I was allowed to go. At one time, our cousin Alvin lived with us while he finished high school. He slept in one of the upstairs rooms. He must have nearly frozen to death that winter, but all I recall of the time he lived with us is his tracing beautiful pictures of animals on thin paper laid across a piece of glass on his lap. He used a light bulb underneath the glass and held between his knees so he could see the outline of the pictures he was tracing. Once Alvin moved out, the upstairs was once again empty of life and not a place we were allowed to go.

However, one day, Linda and I decided to take a look at Mother's ribbon collection and disobeyed the rule of staying out of the upstairs. When we reached the upstairs room and opened the boxes, those strips of colorful satin were much prettier than we had imagined. Naturally, we wanted to share their beauty. We gathered up an assortment and opened the door to the balcony. Making sure we didn't go out, we heaved several armloads of ribbons out onto the roof so the world could see and enjoy. See them they did -- and one observer called my mother. I am not sure I had ever seen her so angry! She grabbed both of us by our arms, dragged us to the kitchen, reached to the top of the refrigerator where she kept a hickory switch at the ready, and proceeded to stripe our legs. Her mantra during all of this was, "I have told you a thousand times to stay out of the upstairs, and what did you do?! What did you do?!" We learned our lesson: the upstairs is off-limits, and disobedience reaps a stiff consequence.

***** I became an official Christian when I was 12 years old. I say official because I never really thought of myself as anything else but a Christian, even when I was just a tiny little girl. But I made it official at age 12. We were in revival at Cross Roads Baptist, and a fellow named James Agan was our pastor. While Mother and Daddy liked him well enough, they always kept him a little at arm's length. He was loud, boisterous, and generally uncouth, and when he got on a roll with his preaching, he loosened his tie, took off his suit jacket and yelled louder than usual. And oh, my, how that man could sweat! In spite of his flamboyant personality, it was he (and not Miss Iner Floyd) who gave me the courage to walk down the aisle and give my life to Jesus. Miss Iner was a widow for as many years as I can remember, and she was forever trying to convert first one and then another of the youth in our church. During the closing hymn, with every head bowed and every eye closed, she often sashayed over to one of us and whispered rather loudly, "I have been praying for you, and I think you are under the conviction." We would squirm and get red-faced, but since none of us quite knew what she meant by being "under the conviction," we didn't respond. However, that evening of revival in the summer of 1957, Preacher Agan passed me on the steps of the church as we were both making our way inside. He stopped beside me, patted me on the head, and said, "I believe you are going to be a wonderful Christian woman one of these days. Do you think you are about ready to get started?" During the closing hymn (probably "Just As I Am"), I left my seat, and with Joelene, Linda, Marian Woodall, and Jean Kay, I walked down the center aisle to make my profession of faith. We were all baptized together the following Sunday. When John and I married and I joined the Methodist church, Cross Roads would not grant me a letter of release to join another denomination, but Rev. Bill Holt, our new pastor at Carrollton First Methodist, said, "Aw, don't worry about them. They are just Baptists holding on to old traditions. We take anybody!" John and I were members number 1000 and 1001, and have continued our Christian journey with those good Methodists ever since.

***** Daddy was a gentle soul. Like the God he worshipped, he was "slow to anger and abounding in steadfast love." He worked long, arduous days in heat and cold and never complained about being the one the rest of us *depended* on regardless of his own *dependability* on *undependable* weather and cotton prices. He rarely said anything negative about his fellow man and would give whatever he had to make life better for those even less fortunate than he. I heard him curse one time. Our bull had gotten into the barn lot when he was supposed to be in the lower pasture. For quite a while, the two of them faced off in a battle of wills. When it finally appeared Daddy had won and was herding the bull toward the gate separating the two parts of the pasture lot, the bull turned and headed toward Daddy instead. With a shout and arms flailing, my father quickly turned the bull around and once again had him on his way, but suddenly the beast made a sharp right turn and started for the back of the barn. Daddy had a pitchfork in his hand that he had been using to urge the bull in the proper direction. When that bull turned the wrong way yet again, Daddy had had it. He threw the pitchfork at the bull; it landed, tines down, on the bull's back and stuck. . . and to my utter astonishment, I heard my father yell, "Damned old bastard!" I, of course, couldn't believe my ears. Daddy said two bad words! Off to the house I ran to report to Mother, but by the time I got there, I had changed my mind. I didn't tell her, and I never mentioned the episode to Daddy, but I think he knew I had heard. After all, as usual, I was right there with him all day as he tried valiantly to keep an eye on me while he went about his daily chores. And most of the time, he whistled and sang and kept his little girls entertained as he worked. Except for that one time.

Sally Jo Bell, 1985

Emmett Bell, 1988

Singular Events:
A New Well and Hog Killin' Time

For four or five years after our family moved to the farm, we drew our drinking water from the hand-dug well outside the pasture fence that surrounded the barn. It never went completely dry, but one year when we again had muddy water for several weeks due to drought, my parents scraped together the funds to put a down payment on a drilled well. What a wonder! And what a day that turned out to be!

Mr. Frank Bishop's heavy trucks and well-drilling equipment rolled into our backyard just after sunrise. It was not long before neighbors began to gather to watch this rare sight. The spot had been marked two days earlier by a dowser, a man who arrived at our house with a Y-shaped hickory stick. He walked all around the yard until he felt the stick bending towards the earth. That's the spot he told Daddy to have Mr. Bishop drill his well. Dowsers are also known as Diviners or Water Witches. Mother was not particularly happy about such a person claiming to find water in this manner. It didn't seem Christian to her, but Daddy believed the man knew what he was doing, and on this particular occasion, he overruled Mother.

The drilling process got started about an hour after the crew arrived. I had never heard such a racket. The engines of the trucks roared, the drill pounded and boomed, and the men hollered so they could be heard above the cacophony. Neighbors came and went and kinfolks dropped by to observe for a spell. This went on hour after hour, but no water. Mother cooked a big dinner (mid-day meal), and the men took turns eating a plate full under the big shade trees. There were several discussions about moving to another location and trying again for water, but Daddy held firm. About 3 o'clock, the drill hit rock. The huge bits had to be changed twice, but finally, in late afternoon, the joyful shout echoed through the air:

"We hit it, we hit it! We got you some water, Mr. Bell!"

And my, oh my, did they ever get us some water. The drill went 183 feet down, into rock, and found a mighty stream. The water was pure and cold and measured at more than five gallons per minute. After the first muddy run-off, our family and the friends and neighbors who had gathered for the event celebrated with tall glasses of the stuff and shared stories of other times and other wells.

To my knowledge, Daddy's well never went dry and the water remained clear and cold, even during the driest of summers. Mother and Daddy used it long after they tapped on to the county water line, a "just-in-case" pipeline that rarely got any use. The tapwater in my home today is certainly potable and usually tasty and cool, but there is nothing that can match the cool, clear water that came from the drilled well in the backyard of our little five-room house in rural Bartow County.

Another exciting time for us occurred every year when the weather turned cold: hog killing time. This annual event took place at the end of November or early December. On hog-killing day, JoEllen and I got to stay out of school if it happened to be a weekday because we were needed to help with the more menial tasks associated with killing hogs. The day had to be really cold so that the meat would not spoil while it was being processed in our backyard.

Like well drilling and chicken catching, this event also started at daybreak. In the backyard, Daddy would start fires around the two big iron wash pots that Mother had filled with bucket after bucket of water. Then Daddy would go down to the barn lot -- WITHOUT JOELLEN AND ME -- to kill the hog he had raised for this purpose. JoEllen and I did not get to witness the killing: Daddy didn't want us exposed to such things. JoEllen would have no doubt been scared that the bullet from the gun would accidently veer off and kill one of us, and I would have cried. Hence, we had to stay in the house with Mother until we heard the shot from Daddy's gun, a weapon that he rarely used except for this purpose.

By this time, several men (called "hands") would have gathered to help with the dressing of the hog. First, Daddy would hitch it to the tractor and drag it up to the backyard. Then, its hind legs were tied together and attached to a block and tackle that had been put on a high limb of a nearby tree. When the men pulled the rope on the block and tackle, the hog was hoisted into the air, its neck was slashed, and the body was drained of blood. I don't remember where the blood went – probably just poured out on the ground and sunk into the soil, an intolerable occurrence for today's environmentalists! Once the bleeding slowed, the belly was split open with a sharp knife, and the bowels were pulled from the inside. It looked disgusting and smelled even worse! I was always amazed at the amount of steam that escaped from the open body cavity when the entrails were pulled out by hand. Some of our neighbors kept the intestines when they killed hogs, cleaned them carefully, and used the casings for sausage. We did not. I think Daddy buried them, but again, I am not sure.

Once the insides of the dead hog were cleared away, the body was hoisted a bit higher, swung around, and then lowered into a clean oil drum that one of the hands had filled with boiling water from the wash pots. Once scalded, the hog was raised in the air again, and the hands maneuvered it over to a long piece of plywood that had been scrubbed thoroughly and laid horizontally at table height on saw horses. The head and feet were cut off and usually given to one of the hands who had come to help. Then, the rest of the hog was scraped down with knives so that every single one of its hairs was removed. Next, it was cut up into pieces. This cutting was true artwork; each part of the hog had to be sectioned in a specific way so that we got the right portions for our pork dinners later in the year.

All the men worked alongside Mother and Daddy to cut away the fat and section off the hams, pork chops, roasts, backbones, ribs, and tenderloin. The smaller, meatier parts that were trimmed from the chops, roasts, hams, and so forth were thrown into clean buckets beside the make-shift table to be ground into sausage, and the fat meat was dropped into separate buckets.

Meanwhile, the wash pot had been partially refilled with fresh water and left to come to a boil again. When the fresh water was boiling, small pieces of fat were thrown in, and my job started. Using an old, worn ax-handle kept year after year for this purpose, I stirred the fat around in the pot to keep it from sticking as it melted away from the skin. This process is called "rendering the lard." I think I got this job because I complained so much about being cold. Standing beside the wash pot certainly kept me warm (and my whining mouth shut). As the fat melted away, the skins cooked to a golden brown, floated to the top, became crispy and curled, and were dipped up for tasty snacks. The melted fat left after the pigskins were removed was strained through cheesecloth into five-gallon, galvanized cans, and after it cooled, it became solid, milky-white lard. The cans were sealed with lids and placed in the smokehouse until needed for cooking later in the year. Some bits of fat that had not melted but had crisped instead were left in the cheesecloth after the straining. These "cracklins" were eaten right off the cheesecloth as a snack or used in cornbread to give it a once-a-year crunch.

Hams had to be separated, trimmed, and salted before being wrapped in burlap and hung in the smokehouse to cure. Daddy had a special recipe that had been passed down from generation to generation for his salt rub. Of course, it was never written down; I suppose that is not such a tragedy since no one I know kills hogs anymore. Our smokehouse had a dirt floor that soaked up the drippings from the ham. I still recall exactly how good it smelled in there! As the other parts were being cut up, Mother was wrapping them in heavy white paper for the freezer or packing them in jars for canning the next day. About half an hour before the work was finished for the day, she would go inside, make biscuits, and fry up some tenderloin. Um-um! That was really good eating. After this meal, the hands helped Daddy clean up outside and went home.

Then, usually after dark, the sausage grinding began. Mother had a little metal grinder with different sized blades that she attached to the white enamel table in our kitchen. She would put small pieces from the buckets into the cup-like opening on the top of the device, turn the handle, and hand grind the meat, adding sage, red and black pepper, and salt. Every few minutes, she would cook a patty to taste for flavor. Sometimes, she would need to add more sage or pepper, but she usually had it just about right the very first time. JoEllen, Daddy, and I were her late-night taste-testers.

Our family ate better at hog-killing time than we did at any other time of the year. The day after the processing day, we always had backbones and ribs for supper. Mother boiled them until they were so tender they fell off the bones. She usually added mashed potatoes, gravy and biscuits, and of course the ever-present green beans. We feasted that day and usually had plenty left over for the next as well. For New Year's Day, we had the required black-eyed peas and turnip greens, but no hog jowl for us. By that time, the cured meat from the previous year was ready, and we had country ham.

Nothing I have ever cooked for my own family, bar none, can compete with those meals we enjoyed on a cold hog-killing day. As I am writing this story, I can see that outside my window is just such a day -- really, really cold. I can almost see the wash pot surrounded by hot coals and smell the smoke rising to the heavens through pine boughs and oak limbs stripped bare of their bounty of autumn leaves. As I reflect on the days gone by, I am really hoping somewhere out there,

there is still a farmer who, like me, is thinking, "What a great day to kill hogs!"

Note: The absence of how to process "chitlins" (more formally called "chitterlings)" may seem like an oversight in this story about hog-killing, but it is not. We never made them and certainly never ate them. Likewise, husband John says his Uncle Bill always had hog brains and eggs for breakfast the day after killing hogs. This meal never graced our Mother's table either. Thank God for small blessings because I am not sure I could have forced myself to swallow either of these two Southern delicacies.

Porches: Echoes of Home

Our front porch was a marvelous spot to spend a few hours of rest and relaxation on a cool summer evening, but during the day, the back porch was the center of activity. When we moved to the house and farm in 1952, our back porch stretched from one rear corner of the house to the other with access from both bedrooms: Mother and Daddy's and the one JoEllen and I shared. The porch was unpainted, unscreened, and had no underpinning and no railings around it or on the six or seven steps that climbed precariously from the ground to the edge of the uneven floorboards. Those steps got extremely slick any time it rained. A couple of years after we moved, Mother fell on them with a dishpan full of wet clothes she was about to hang out on the line, so Daddy scrounged up some old asphalt shingles from somewhere and nailed them to the treads for traction. The north end of the porch was only a few inches off the ground, but the slope of the backyard meant that the south end was elevated about five feet. JoEllen and I had a good time seeing which one could land the farthest out in the grass when we jumped off this end of the porch. That is, until Daddy caught us and promptly stopped his work long enough to nail up some makeshift railings and warn us to never climb under, between, or over the rails, or he would "skin up alive." We believed him.

Mother's wringer washing machine stood on the north end of the back porch. From there, we could see across the dirt driveway to the wash pot: a large, black iron kettle that held 15-18 gallons of water. Its feet sat on a couple of rocks so that the pot was off the ground enough to build a fire under and around it to heat the water. On wash day, Daddy built a fire early so that by mid-morning, Mother could tote buckets of boiling water to the machine for her laundry. Clothes were all washed in the same water but in a particular order: whites first, then coloreds, then Daddy's work clothes. The wash water was increased and warmed up between loads with another bucket or two of water from the wash pot. When the clothes had agitated as long as Mother deemed necessary, she would wring them out a bit by hand, then pass them through the rollers on the wringer at the top of the machine to get out more water. The clothes dropped from the wringer into a zinc tub of cold water on the other side of the washing machine for their first rinse. The wringer part of the machine had a knob on top above the rollers that could be loosened so that this entire part could be swung out to a 45 degree angle. Once the wringer was turned and secured, it sat between the first tub of rinse water and a second one next to it. The clothes in the first rinse were passed through the wringer again and into the second rinse. The same process happened again when the wringer was moved to its third position; clothes left the second rinse, went through the wringer, and dropped into a large dishpan on the other side ready to be hung on the clothesline. The line was a wire strung tightly from two wooden posts about twenty feet apart with a support post in the middle. I heard Mother brag on Daddy many times about his "always keeping a good taunt clothesline up and ready." Like the order of the actual washing, she also had a strict regimen for hanging out the clothes. First, the line had to be cleaned with a wet rag. Then items had to be hung by category: towels together, sheets together, blouses together, and so on. And clothes could not EVER be thrown over the line. Mother thought this method for hanging clothes was "common." Our clothes were hung by the edges. Sheets were folded, and the open ends were pinned to the line in three places with the fold at the bottom. Blouses were hung by the hems, dresses by the shoulders, towels and washrags by the edges. Only Daddy's overalls could be across the line where the bib met the waist, and that was only because they would have dragged the ground if hung otherwise. On very cold days, the wash froze on the line. Mother would bring her stiff laundry inside in the late afternoon and dry it by the fireplace or wood heater, batch by batch, on the backs of the kitchen chairs set close to the source of heat.

The other end of the back porch, our jumping off end, overlooked the side yard with the dirt driveway on the right running about 500 yards down to Mansfield Road. From our spot on the porch, we could see Mother drawing water from the well across the road, or watch Daddy going about his tasks in the barn lot. We could see the occasional car or truck headed north in a cloud of dust from the direction of our nearest neighbors, Mr. and Mrs. Tatum, but we could not see their house because it sat about three-quarters of a mile away and was hidden by a stand of trees. We could see the chicken coup across the road from the well: an open-air, two-story roosting structure for our yard chickens. Beyond the coop and up the hill inside the pasture fence stood a three-room relic of a house that was once a tenant dwelling but which Daddy used to store hay and a few farm implements. Once, when he was "down on his luck," Daddy's brother F.M. and his wife Barbara cleaned it out and lived in it for several months until he could get back on his feet. The place had no electricity or running water, a two-eye wood stove for cooking, and little else. I do not know how they managed, but they did for a little while until they found a place in White.

JoEllen and I observed all of this from our perch on the back porch and made up stories to go with everything we saw. We even named the scarecrows in the garden across the driveway and behind the smokehouse, and we often dreamed of them coming to life and scaring something besides crows.

Perhaps the most unusual memory I have of that back porch is more than a little strange, perhaps even outrageous, to present-day readers. The jumping contest was not the only competition JoEllen and I concocted. We also learned to pull our panties down, squat at the edge of the porch, and see which of us could pee the farthest out into the yard! What a way for little girls to entertain themselves! Of course, this contest was always at night. When it was daylight, we used the toilet. Some of our friends and relatives called this al fresco restroom the outhouse, but we never did. Probably, it was thought to be "common" to use such words.

Other things in our everyday lives were also rude or crude or "common" and were not spoken of in front of company. While Daddy was much too easy on us and would have allowed us to say or do almost anything as long as we didn't get hurt or hurt someone else, Mother somehow knew that she needed to teach us some lessons about manners and behavior if we were to manage in an adult world. Many of those lessons were learned while the three of us sat on one of the porches, stringing beans, peeling peaches, or shelling peas. With only a high school education and little worldly experience, our mother must have spent many hours late at night reading about proper etiquette and some of the finer things in life in the few magazines she could afford. Ladies, she told us, did not curse -- EVER.

Ladies did not drink liquor or smoke cigarettes. Ladies did not say the N word. We did not whine. We did not beg. We did not wear our skirts too short or too tight. We did not pop our gum when we were lucky enough to have some. We did not complain; there were plenty of other folks in the world who were in worse shape than we were. We wrote thank you notes when someone gave us a gift or showed us some special attention. We did not bite our nails or slump our shoulders. We were to always "stand up straight and act like we had good sense." I don't remember that I appreciated these crucial lessons at the time, but now I am truly grateful that my mother took the time and effort to instill them in her girls.

The fun and games and the special lessons we two little girls learned out on the porch when we lived in our rickety clapboard house with a view of the Blue Ridge mountains may not be the sort that others believe to be the consummate education, but our lessons were filled to the top with unconditional love from both a mother and a father whose character was untainted and whose faith in God has sustained us all of our days. It only takes a little nudge to send the two of us floating on a cloud of memory, hearing the echoes of home with its joy, laughter, and singing while we sat out on the porch on a cool summer evening -- just the four of us.

The stories that follow are by JoEllen Bell Wilson. We did not collaborate about the content; all the stories in this collection, mine and hers, were written independently. Our memories are set in the same time and place, include the same people and events, and are remembered with the same abiding love of family and rural life. They are, like the two of us, essentially the same stories
   . . . yet, somehow, they are different.

Whippings

Daddy never whipped Anne. He only whipped me once.

Perhaps you should know what a 'whipping' is; It is when a child under 12 years old does something naughty and the Mother and/or Daddy gives them a spanking. . .in the country we call it a 'whipping'.

A whipping at our house was given by Mother for many types of indiscretions. If you were caught telling a falsehood, such as "Oh no, I didn't throw rocks at the cows . . .or getting your cousin Lint into trouble (telling him to walk in the mud in his new shoes . . or shooting your sister with a BB gun (I shot her twice: once in the heel – an accident . . and once in the back – because she kept running in front of my target!).

Mother would tell us to go outside and get a switch (a small branch from a bush or tree limb). If we didn't get one *keen* enough (one that would hurt really badly when it struck your bare legs), Mother would get one for us – and believe me – you did not want her to choose the switch!

She would then proceed to hold you by one arm and hit bare legs with the switch about 10 times (it seemed like 100 times). When she let go, you were crying hysterically and your legs (and feelings) HURT! I can remember feeling very guilty for whatever I'd done long after the bodily pain subsided. So much for Baptist upbringing – if you didn't know better, you'd think we had some Jewish blood. I received many whippings – but I do want to explain the 3 times I remember very vividly:

> 1. I was always day-dreaming – about everything. One day I climbed on the gate that led into the barn lot after piling up about 8 or 9 rocks. These rocks represented my arsenal for the 'bad guys' (cows just minding their own business walking around the lot). As a cow would come from behind the barn, I would let him or her have it! Sometimes I hit one – most times I missed. But, in my mind, I was killing the enemy. Mother just happened to come on the front porch and saw what I was doing. She was thinking that in an hour or two, Daddy would arrive at the barn to milk the cows. Mother did not want to help him run down scared cows to get them in the stable or to dress a kick on the leg from an angry cow. "JoEllen, get me a switch!" No more day-dreaming. I got the real thing!

2. Lint and Brenda Gail are our cousins who lived closest to us. We either went to their house, or they came to our house about once a week. They are Aunt Ruth and Uncle Sidney's children. Brenda Gail is 3 years younger than Anne and Lint is about a year younger than Anne – or four years younger than me. One day when they came over, Aunt Ruth had them dressed up for another visit somewhere else. They were just stopping by our house for a few minutes. It had rained and when that occurred, we had some really great red mud in our driveway and down our road. We were playing dodgeball in the (safe) grass, when our ball rolled into the road. I told Lint, since was the only boy, he should retrieve our ball. Lint would do anything – and I knew it! He ran right out into the mud and his beautifully shined shoes were ruined! We tried to wash them off with the hose, but he got real wet and finally, I just told him to go get in the car and wait for his mother. After they left, Aunt Ruth found out what happened. And soon, Mother called out, "JoEllen, get me a switch!"

3. I do not remember why Mother and Daddy got me a BB gun. Daddy was always so worried about every little thing that I cannot fathom how he could agree to a BB gun. But, he did and the first day I got

it, I set up a target in the back yard to practice my shooting. I was about 8 – so Anne was 5. She was interested in watching me shoot – and walked between me and the target - just as I pulled the trigger. My aim was off – and I got her in the heel. It was really pretty awful – all swollen and red. She got fixed up with a bandage and we went back outside. Soon, she began to ask if she could shoot the gun. I told her, "No, you're too little." She kept bugging me and I thought I'd just shoot behind her to scare her a bit. Again, my aim was off and I shot her in the back. Within one minute, I heard, "JoEllen, get me a switch!" That was my last day with a BB gun.

As to why Daddy never whipped Anne and only whipped me once. . . .he had his own methods. If we behaved badly, he would give us a **look**, which would hurt to the core! We felt hurt, guilty, chastised and mortified. His other method was more physical. He would thump us behind the ear. If you got an ear-thump, you knew Daddy meant business and we would stop whatever we were doing IMMEDIATELY. I do believe he could lean over 4 benches in church and give me an ear-thump. No more talking, giggling or reading *Home Life* instead of listening to the preacher. I'd rather get a whipping from Mother any day than a *look* or ear-thump from Daddy. Go figure.

Reunions

Getting together with family was one of the highlights of our life. Social events centered on the Church and Reunions ran a close second.

Our family, both the Bells and Lipscombs, were large when compared to today's klans.

Daddy had a twin sister, Corene, another sister, Aunt Elmer (we changed that to Aunt Elma - Sounds much more sophisticated!) brothers, Uncle Dick, Uncle Robert and F.M. (we never called F.M. 'uncle'. . .)

Mother's sisters were Aunt Edythe and Aunt Ruth, brothers were Uncle Nathan, Uncle Will, Uncle Harry and Uncle Walt. All brothers all served in WWII, 3 were overseas (Uncle Walt did not go overseas) and everyone came home without a scratch! Big Mama's prayers were answered.

Daddy and Uncle Dick were farmers and they did not have to go to War; Uncle Robert was a Railroad man, who was spared War service; but F.M. was in the Army.

We lived just a block (a few yards – in the country, 'block' was not something of measurement) from Granny and Granddad and Dean (Corene), so we visited them <u>every</u> night. Daddy would carry Anne, until her feet drug the ground and I would hop, skip, run and walk beside him asking questions every moment, as we went for a nightly visit. Dean would brush our hair, while Daddy talked with Granny and Granddad. Mother stayed home. She wasn't much to visit Daddy's folks.

We went to Big Mama Lipscomb's EVERY Sunday. . . .after Church. Three of Mother's brothers and families and Aunt Ruth and family and cousin Wesley were there. Aunt Edythe, Uncle Frank, Judy and Jackie Fran and Uncle Nathan, Aunt Sarah, Joey and Beth lived in Atlanta (!!) and weren't 'regular'. Mother, Daddy, Anne and me, Uncle Harry, Aunt Sara Nell, Linda, Steve, Gary and Big Mama were members at Wofford's Cross Roads Baptist Church (and were there if the doors were open). Aunt Ruth, Uncle Sidney, Lint and Brenda Gail belonged to Bartow Presbyterian Church. (Cross Roads Baptist wouldn't send Aunt Ruth's 'letter' to a Presbyterian Church and 'turned her out' for joining this denomination! Cross Roads also refused to give Anne her 'letter', when she joined a United Methodist Church after she married). Uncle Will, Aunt Vera, Stanley and Veda belonged to Gilmer Street Baptist in Cartersville. Uncle Walt, Aunt Jimmye, Melodye and Holly belonged to Cartersville First Baptist, where Aunt Jimmye was Choir Director.

Around 12:30 p.m., we would all gather at Big Mama's for dinner (lunch, nowadays). Everyone brought something for the meal and we'd eat around 1 p.m. After lunch, sisters and sisters-in-law, brothers and brothers-in-law, and Wesley, (Aunt Edithe's oldest lived with Big Mama after he left Berry High School and became like 'one of the brothers', instead of a grandson) would all sit either in the living room (in winter) or on the porch (in summer) to talk. All the kids would play together, except me, the oldest granddaughter - - I was in the kitchen with Big Mama, washing dishes.

These get-togethers were semi-reunions. Because they happened, either daily or weekly, we did not consider them official 'Reunions'.

GrandDad Bell was the only boy with 5 sisters. Our great-aunts lived in Marietta – and away from Bartow County, so we did not see them often.

GrandDad and Granny had 6 children.

The Bells had close family Reunions, at which Daddy's sisters, brothers and all their kids and grandkids would gather, usually at our house. We had no particular day, just whenever Daddy would decide it was time to see everybody. Everyone lived in Bartow County, except Aunt Elma and Uncle Ernest who lived in Etowah, Tennessee- - -so we only saw them at Reunions. . .or when Daddy would let Anne and me ride the Greyhound Bus to Etowah for a visit. They brought Mary and twins Jane and Wayne. Uncle Dick and Aunt Evie brought Bobby, Kat, Alvin, Opal, Nancy, Andy and Syble. F.M. and Barbara brought Debbie, Daryl and Sharon. Uncle Robert and Aunt Marie brought Howell. Dean was an 'ole maid' (no political correctness then) so she claimed all her nieces and nephews as her 'chilluns'. (Anne and I were her favorites!!)

As always, there was plenty of food, lots of kids playing and many 'tall tales'.

The Big Lipscomb Reunion was an annual affair on the 4th of July each year. They occurred at Uncle Herschel's home .

Uncle Herschel was one of Daddy Lint Lipscomb's 6 brothers. In addition, there were 4 sisters born to the Family of Nathan LaFayette and Laura Lieuraney Crowe Lipscomb. All 11 children had large families - - and with 1st, 2nd, 3rd cousins and other random relatives, we'd usually have about 200 people!

Uncle Herschel lived on a large farm, that would accommodate about 100 – 200 people each summer. It was always HOT. Uncle Herschel and Aunt Ethel would either stretch chicken wire between trees and/or put plywood on sawhorses and cover with tablecloths to accommodate all the food. Each family brought a BASKET filled with food. You've NEVER seen so much food! Fried Chicken, Baked Hams, Roast Beef, every vegetable imaginable (some even cooked into 'casseroles'!), salads and Lordy – beautiful DESSERTS! The women-kin cooked for DAYS to bring a suitable basket to The Reunion!

The women put out the food, the men talked, the children ran, jumped and played around the **Spring with no bottom**!

There was a beautiful creek meandering along Uncle Herschel's farm, that began in a large [water] Spring and included a 'SpringHouse', which housed milk, butter, etc. in years past. THE SPRING HAD NO BOTTOM!! Daddy would remind Anne and me about this natural phenomenon each year, since there was no fence around The Spring and it was very close to the food tables. I watched Anne like a hawk, because I knew if she fell in, she'd likely end up in China or some such foreign place and we'd never see her again!

I've since learned there are actually natural springs with no apparent bottoms located here in the South. . . .but, at Uncle Herschel's - - all us children KNEW his Spring was a dangerous thing and we did not get close enough to put even a toe in the cool, cool water! We did, however, wade in the cool creek behind the springhouse.

The Lipscomb Kin still meet today and we'll have about 50 – 100 people. But, now, we need an air-conditioned building. Children play indoor games and no one worries about falling into The Spring. Somehow, it's just not the same.

Granny and Granddad's Family
Front: Corene, Fred and Lena Bell, Elma
Back: Dick, Rob, F.M., Emmett

Big Mama's Family
Front: Will, Nida Collins Lipscomb, Nathan
Back: Harry, Edythe, Sally Jo, Ruth, Walt

Medicine

I'm not sure if it was the clean air, the good food, the healthy life-style or just pure luck – but none of us was sick often. We would have an occasional bad-cold and Anne and I had measles, mumps and chicken pox, but otherwise, we were a healthy family.

Perhaps left over from his own upbringing, Daddy was adamant about giving us the requisite potion for cleaning out our systems. . .whether needed or not.

About twice a year, after supper, he would come into the Living Room (in winter) or on the Porch (in summer), with a little pill. Honestly, that thing was so minuscule it was hardly visible with the naked eye. But, oh my, I can still remember the taste. It was horrible – not to mention how it made you feel the next day. He called it a 'ca-ladril'. We endured, because he was so sure that if we didn't take it, we might get sick. Talk about healthy life-style, I wonder how my grandchildren would react to the dreaded caladril.

An outstanding memory of being sick is when I had the measles. I was really sick. Big Mama lived with us in the big house in White. (For a time, she and Wesley lived in the front room of that house - - but I have no idea why!). We borrowed a hospital bed from the Church and it was set up in the living room for me. For about a week, I just laid there, with a high fever and I don't remember much. When I started feeling a little better, Big Mama gave me a package of margarine that had a small red pouch in the corner that was used to color the shortening. Again, I have no idea why, but even then marketing was on the cutting edge. I manipulated, squeezed and stroked those several packages of margarine, until they looked like real butter. This gave me something to do to while away the boring hours of lying in bed. Today's equivalent of a laptop – or whatever technology is popular.

Of course, the biggest worry-wart of all time was Daddy. He couldn't stand for Anne or me to be sick and would do anything we asked or hinted about to make us smile.

Before I came down with measles, I had spied a pair of bunny bedroom slippers in a store in Cartersville that I wanted very, very much. But they were too expensive to purchase for wearing only in the house, so my dreams of bunny bedroom slippers died. UNTIL I got the measles!

My fever had spiked and Daddy came into the room with an aspirin and a bottle of co-cola. I hated taking aspirin almost as much as caladril. He said, "I'm going to grind up this little aspirin into a spoon full of co-cola. You won't even taste it." I wasn't buying that. Then he said the magic words. "If you'll take this little ole aspirin, with co-cola, when you feel better, we'll go to town and buy you those little bunny bedroom slippers." My eyes closed, my mouth opened and I swallowed the awful co-cola diluted aspirin. I got better within a day or two and sure enough, Daddy and I went to town and I wore my bunny bedrooms home. Anne got them after I outgrew them, but she didn't have to work as hard for them as I did.

Another time of *taking medicine* noteworthy in my life was the year I stopped by Granny and Granddad's house on my way home from school to receive a daily dose of *Hadicol*. This was an advertised, over the counter liquid that helped boost an appetite in order to gain weight. Not even imaginable today. Anyway, I had always been a skinny little girl. And, when compared to Anne; the beautiful, blonde, blue-eyed, light-skinned, perfect size little girl, I was a mess! Skinny, frizzy hair, dark and gangly. Granny and Dean thought they could improve on my looks, if they could help me gain a little weight. Mother didn't question that I was stopping by their house each day, since it was on my way home from school. She probably thought I was getting a cookie and milk after a long day of studying. Nooooo. Granny would be ready when I walked in the door, with a spoon and the bottle. Dean was the instigator and Granny carried out the duty. It really didn't taste so bad and I *did* get a cookie and milk after. I guess I took 2 or 3 bottles before Mother found out (probably, it slipped out. I was never good at keeping secrets). Mother forbid me to take one more drop - - you see, an ingredient in Hadicol was ALCOHOL. That was a forbidden drug at our house, even in the form of a teaspoon a day. I don't know how Mother and Daddy resolved* the dilemma of me visiting Granny after school. I just remember that when I did, no more medicine!

*I must add that I NEVER heard my Mother and Daddy argue. When I first met John's parents, I went on a road-trip with them and they argued all the way from Atlanta to Augusta. I was horrified! I honestly did not know married adults ever had a cross word between them. And, you won't believe this: Anne and I are in our 70s and we have NEVER had a disagreement. Just not in our DNA.

P.S. John and I have had many arguments. I guess I went over to the 'dark side' with him!

APPENDIX

Terminology, Almost Extinct Items, and Other Oddities

1. BLUE HORSES. The outside band around every new pack of notebook paper from the Montag paper company featured a picture of the head of a blue horse that could be cut out and saved until the collector had enough to "buy" an item of her dreams, such as a Brownie camera or a cap pistol. Green stamps from the grocery store worked the same way.
2. BOBBY PINS. Black, brown, or grey hairpins about 1/16 inch wide by two inches long with one straight side and one corrugated side that clamp together to hold hair in place. For years, I parted my hair on the left side and used a bobby pin on the right to hold the bangs in place.
3. BOBBY SOCKS. Thick white socks for girls worn with cuffs rolled down two turns. When JoEllen was in high school, she sometimes used a second sock wound around and under the cuff to make it as thick as possible. I guess that made the socks more attractive??
4. BOY-HIDEY. Exclamation of joy, as in "Boy-Hidey, we just had a good shower of rain!"
5. BUCKET CANDY. Single pieces of candy, sometimes with a wrapper, that came in big buckets and sold in a general merchandise store

for a penny or perhaps two for a penny. Daniels' store had lots of bucket candy! My favorite was the jellied orange slice. JoEllen preferred Mary Janes.

6. BUTCHER KNIVES. Large, usually nickel-plated knives with wooden handles used especially during hog killing. Every home had at least three of these knives that stayed in the back of the knife drawer until hog-killing and had to be cleaned before use due to rust.
7. CAUTION. Really unusual, as in "Ain't he a caution!"
8. DINNER ON THE GROUND(S). Any outdoor meal at the church which moved inside to the basement or fellowship hall in inclement weather.
9. D'RECKLY. Directly or very soon, as in "I will be there d'reckly."
10. FAIR TO MIDDLIN'. Average. After his stroke, when asked how he was feeling, Daddy would always say "fair to middlin" or "tolerable," even when he felt rather miserable. The term "fair to middlin" comes from cattle auctions where cows were graded as Fair, Middle-Grade [middlin], or Good, hence, "fair to middlin" meant not bad, but not too good either.
11. FARE THEE WELL. To the utmost – one often performed a task to a fare-thee-well (better than anyone else).
12. FEATURE. Beyond understanding, as in "Cleve says he ain't up to putting in a crop this year --can you feature that?'

13. FLESHENED UP. Put on weight, as in "I do believe Bessie has fleshened up since last Camp Meeting."
14. GOIN' TO TOWN. In a hurry but still competent, as in "She is really goin' to town sewing that dress."
15. GUANO. A type of fertilizer that we pronounced as "gwoo AN er" with the accent on the second syllable. Mother sometimes made our clothes out of "gwooaner" sacks.
16. HOMEPLACE. A farm owned and operated by the same family for several generations. The Lipscomb homeplace and the Bell homeplace are both in Bartow County, Georgia.
17. I'LL BE JOHN BROWN. Exclamation of astonishment, as in, "Well, I'll be John Brown if that Wesley didn't drive Big Mama's car to church but forgot to bring Big Mama!"
18. I'LL SWAN or I'LL SWANNIE. Exclamation of amazement. If someone happens to have triplets, Mother might say, "Well, I'll swan. She didn't look like she was going to have a litter!"
19. IT'S COMING UP A CLOUD. It is going to rain, probably with lightning and thunder.
20. LAYING-BY TIME. A few weeks in mid to late August when the cotton has been hoed for the last time, the vegetable garden is waning, and there is little to do in the field except wait for cotton pickin' time; hence, all is "laid by" for a brief time of rest and repair. Annual Camp Meeting services at the nearby Pine

Log Methodist Church were usually scheduled so that they occurred during laying-by time.

21. LIKE TO DIED. Became breathless with laughter, scorn, or embarrassment, as in "When I saw she was wearing the same hat I had on my head for Easter services, I like to died!"
22. LONG-HEAD. Our father's favorite term for JoEllen when she did something crazy, like driving our '50-model Plymouth into the septic tank he was digging with a pick and shovel in the backyard.
23. NARY-UN. Not one, as in "Can I borrow a pencil; I ain't got nary-un."
24. NED. Someone not very far up the food chain economically, socially, or culturally. Only a true country girl, perhaps only one kin to the Bell kids, recognizes a NED.
25. NOUGHT. Zero as in 19+1=20, so when you add, put down your nought and carry your 1.
26. PAPER POKE. Brown paper sack, usually the smaller ones used for bucket candy and other small items like bolts and screws purchased at a general merchandise store.
27. PENNY LOAFERS. The same ones still seen today except that we kept ours shined to a "fare thee well" and wore shiny copper pennies in the slots – I put dimes in mine just to get attention!
28. RENCH. Rinse, as in "Rench off your hands before you eat."

29. SHE CAME WITHIN A PEA OF DYING. She was very sick.
30. SLOP. Left-over food scraps saved in a slop bucket for the pigs.
31. SNOT NOSE. An obnoxious child. "That snot-nose kid just stole my book satchel!"
32. SOFT-TOE BALLERINAS. Girls' very thin-soled, soft leather black shoes with no heels. The top of the toe was pleated and adorned with a tiny bow. Girls always wore bobby socks with their soft-toe ballerinas.
33. SOMMERS. Somewhere, as in "That pencil is around here sommers."
34. SPELL. 1. a short period of time, perhaps an hour or so, as in "Why don't you come on up here on the porch and set a spell?" 2. a brief incident of illness, especially mental or emotional trauma, as in "She looked like she was having a spell, but then she perked right back up."
35. SWORD DRILL. Oral Bible quiz. The object of the game is to be the first person to find a named scripture passage, such as John 3:16. With each round, the person who is last to find the passage must sit down, and the last person standing is the winner. Participants line up side by side. When the leader calls out "Attention," the participants hold their closed Bibles in one hand with arms at their sides. Next, the leader says, "Draw swords!" and the participants extend their Bibles in front of them, left hand on the bottom and right hand on the top. When the

leader says, "Salute!" players open their Bibles. Finally, the leader calls out the verse and chapter and says, "Charge!" The participants turn to the passage and shout "Got it!" The passage is then read aloud for correctness. The last person to find the passage sits down, and the next round begins. The winner is the last one standing. There is often heated debate about which person was the last to find the passage. (NOTE: I adored sword drills!)

36. TIGHT-TAIL SKIRT. Straight, body-hugging skirt with a kick-pleat in the back. A few girls wore theirs _too_ tight and were in danger of losing their good reputations.
37. TOLERABLE. Feeling all right but not excellent. After Daddy had his stroke, his standard answer to any question about his well-being was, "Tolerable, tolerable."
38. TWO SHAKES OF A SHEEP'S TAIL. As fast as possible. "I will be there in two shakes of a sheep's tail."
39. UGLY. Behaving or speaking in a rude, vulgar, or otherwise unacceptable fashion, as in "Miss Thelma just could not abide children who acted ugly or used ugly words."
40. USE'TA COULD. Was once able to, as in "I use'ta could turn cartwheels."

Family

The Bells
Thomas North Epps *married* Cecelia Penelope Jennings.* They had several children including Sallie Selena. Sallie Selena Epps (against the wishes of her father)** *married* Richard Bledsoe Bell. They had daughters Estelle, Lucy, Jessie, Kate, Ann, Claire, and Mildred, but their only son was named **Fred Moten**.

About the same time, James Goss *married* Carrie Rebecca Hannah. They had two daughters, Ada and **Mary Lena**. When Carrie Rebecca died, James married Era Mae Henson. They had one son, James Goss.

Fred Moten Bell *married* **Mary Lena Goss**. Their children were Richard Bledsoe, Elma Hampton, **James Emmett**, Jesse Corene, Fred Moten, Jr., and Robert Thurston.

James Emmett Bell *married* **Sally Jo Lipscomb** (1937). They had two daughters, **JoEllen** (1942) and **Ruth Anne** (1945).

JoEllen Bell *married* **John Henry Wilson** (1961), and they had twin sons, James Elliot and John Emmett (October 13, 1967)

James Elliot Wilson *married/divorced* Claudia Picone, and they had Rachel Anna Wilson and Matthew James Wilson.

John Emmett Wilson *married/divorced* Haley Bledsoe, and they had Aleczander Carter Wilson and Samuel Kyle Wilson. Johnny married Debbie (Ely) in 2021.

Ruth Anne Bell *married* **John Luther Ball** (1966) and they had a son David Christopher (Aug. 8, 1967) and a daughter Janet Lynn (Oct. 17, 1970). David Christopher Ball *married* Shannon Leigh Watson. Their three sons are David Christopher Ball, Jr., William Watson Ball, and Joseph McCranie Ball

Janet Lynn Ball *married* Richard Martin Geriner, Jr. Their three sons are Richard Martin Geriner, III (Tripp), John Carter Geriner, and Holden Butler Geriner.

Information is from Janice Goss Sherrouse in her genealogy of the Bell/Goss family.
** Family lore.

The Lipscombs

William Henry Collins *married* Mary Matilda Mahan. They had **Mary Nida**, John Franklin, Cola Rebecca, Willie Sue, Robert Lee, Ira L., and Nala Mae. About the same time, Nathan LaFayette Lipscomb *married* Laura Lieuraney Crow. They had Oscar, Ethel, Jim, Kit, **Lint**, Tom, Maggie, Minnie, Rob, Hershel, and Fannie.

Mary Nida Collins *married* **Joseph Linton Lipscomb**. They had Edythe Linton, Ruth Collins, **Sally Jo**, Nathan LaFayette, Will Henry, Harry Melvin, and Walter Daniel.

Sally Jo Lipscomb *married* **James Emmett Bell**.

Descendants of this union are listed above in Bell family.

Bell Cousins

Elma's children with Ernest Price

Mary (deceased) husband Gene Hayes (deceased), children Linda and Leslie

Jane (deceased) -- daughter Tracey with 1st husband C.H. Lee (deceased), and son Mark with 2nd husband Robert Gregg

Wayne (deceased) – wife Ann, daughters Scottie & Shelby; second wife Tootsie, son Greg

Dick's children with Evvie (Martin)

Bobby (deceased) – wife Geraldine (deceased), children Wanda Sue and Randal (deceased)

Alvin (deceased) –wife Pete (deceased), children Kim, Jill, and Ritchie (deceased)

Katherine (Kat) – husband Brad Lipscomb (deceased), son Davey (deceased)

Opal – husband Frank Sligh (deceased), no children

Nancy (deceased) – husband Charles Morris (deceased), no children

Andy – wife Jean, son Russell

Syble (deceased) -- husband Greg Reed, son Alex

F.M.'s children with Barbara (Stewart)

Debbie – husband Harry Martin, sons Brandon (deceased), Blake, and Jason

Sharon – son Kenneth (KC) with former husband James Frith

Daryl -- wife Molina (deceased), no children

Robert's child with Marie (Nelson)

Howell (deceased) – wife Nancy (deceased), sons Chris, Eric, and Rob

Lipscomb Cousins

<u>Edythe's children with Frank Hann</u>

Wesley – wife LaTrelle, sons Derek and Devin

Judy -- husband Lamar Cash (deceased), son Brad, daughters with 1st husband "Gator" Ayers: Renee and Steve Ann

Jackie -- husband Henry Collins, daughter Jill; son with Johnny Hester: Tommy; son and daughter with Ronnie Perkins: Billy and Lisa

<u>Ruth's children with Sidney Stegall</u>

Lint – wife Sandra, sons Sidney and Joseph

Brenda Gail – husband Henry Tyson, daughters Summer and Sunday

<u>Sally Jo's children with Emmett Bell</u>

JoEllen -- husband John Henry Wilson, twin sons Jimmy and Johnny

Anne -- husband John Ball, son David and daughter Janet

Nathan's children with Sara (Williams)

Joey (deceased) wife Wendy, daughter Nicole

Beth – husband Tim Moon, children with 1st husband Bob McCarthy: Lauren & Jenna; stepchildren with Tim

Will's children with Vera (Vaughan)

Stanley (deceased) – daughter Vaughan (with former wife Rose)

Veda – husband James Hilton (deceased), daughter Alisha, son Drew

Harry's children with Sara Nell (Carpenter)

Linda – husband Pete Goodrich, children Patrick, Ryan, and Blaine

Steve – wife Robyn (deceased), son Ian; 2nd wife Christine

Gary – wife Lisa, no children

Walt's children with Jimmye (Hegwood)

Melody – husband Gary Thacker, sons Terry (Gary's), Cary, and Dan

Holly -- husband Dan Guilliam, daughter Sara with 1st husband Pete Perry; step-children with Dan

Births/Deaths

Joseph Linton Lipscomb	11-30-1882/1947
Mary Nida (Collins) Lipscomb	7-14-1891/3-2-1996
Fred Moten Bell, Sr	11-12-1881/1-25-1966
Mary Lena (Goss) Bell	2-15-1882/3-10-1965
James Emmett Bell	10-15-1909/8-16-1997
Sally Jo (Lipscomb) Bell	2-13-1917/4-19-2004
Jesse Corene Bell	1909 / 1996
Richard Bledsoe Bell II	1908 / 1979
Robert Thurston Bell	1918 / 2005
Fred Moten Bell, Jr.	1916 / 1997
Elma Hampton Bell Price	1906 / 1995
Edythe Lipscomb Hann	1914 / 2002
Ruth Collins Lipscomb Stegall	1915 / 2009
Nathan LaFayette Lipscomb	1918 / 1993
Will Henry Lipscomb	1921 / 2000
Harry Melvin Lipscomb	1925 / 2013
Walter Daniel Lipscomb	1928 / 2013

And just in case you are wondering...

I started jotting down my memories of childhood when Mother began to lose her own memory. I did not think at the time that I would eventually end up with this little book. In fact, writing down how I was feeling and what I remembered was mostly a way to deal with the sadness of watching Mother's decline. I destroyed many of my musings because, once committed to paper, they had done their cathartic job. But somewhere along the way, I realized that you -- my children, my grandchildren, and any of my extended family and friends who happen to read my stories -- might enjoy learning of what it was like to grow up during that period of time in recent history when there was no war, politicians were respected members of society, there was very little civil unrest, and we had enough family, religious, and community spirit to share with those around us. It was truly an idyllic time.

I never fancied myself a writer at all. I loved teaching others to put their thoughts on paper, to organize their words and sentences in a way that would appeal to their readers, and to help them gain a sense of accomplishing a task they once thought they could not do. My own writing was confined to putting together examples of various kinds of writing to demonstrate the end product to my students. I have not ever wanted to write "the great American novel," and my poetic talents are quite limited. I am including only one poem.

It was written shortly after John and I returned from our adventure on a sailboat in the Caribbean with cousins Brenda Gail and Henry.

Each of the stories included here began as a mere fragment of thought, but as I began to write about that fragment, another part of the story would reveal itself, and then another and then another until a full and vivid picture came into view. At least that is what happened most of the time. In the chapter called "In the Corners of My Mind," you can read some of the fragments that I wanted to share but which never quite filled out into complete stories.

One story I do not know and regret not having asked about is how my parents met and how Daddy proposed to Mother, if indeed he did. Knowing the two of them, it may have been the other way around. Alas, I never asked. And since you, my children, have not asked about how your parents met, here is the story that didn't fit in anywhere else in this book but which I think you might want to know . . . eventually.

When I was a freshman at West Georgia College (now known as the University of West Georgia), I was dating a boy back home named Randal Lowery. He was a year younger than I, so he was still in high school. We had talked seriously of marriage and a future together. I did not have a car, so the only times I went home to see him were when Joelene, my best friend forever, jumped in the Blue Goose (her 1960 Ford Fairlane) and headed to White with me riding shotgun. The old saw that "absence makes the heart grow fonder" did not happen in my case; instead, it was more like "out of sight, out of mind." My eyes and heart began to wander, and I began to date other people, notably a young man from West Point, Georgia, named Jesse Lancaster. One of his friends, a blonde, blue-eyed "boy" of 23, also began appearing from time to time. One day my friend Kathy Wolfe arranged a blind date for me to go out with the blonde. She said he would pick me up in front of our dormitory at 7, but she did not tell me anything else, not even his name. At the appointed time, I was watching when the blonde drove up in his little Fiat, jumped the one-brick-high curbing, and parked on the porch of Mandeville Hall. He came inside, and asked our house mother to let me know he had arrived for our date. I came downstairs, we exchanged names, went to a movie, and then to the A & W drive-in restaurant for a burger and root beer. When I got back to my dormitory, the upstairs windows were filled with the anxious faces of a multitude of my friends and dorm mates who were eagerly awaiting my return, hoping I would get back all right. What Kathy had conveniently failed to tell me was that the blonde had a terrible reputation. He dated and dropped girls; he rarely went to class; he drove too fast (and parked anyplace the Fiat would fit); he got into fights; and he drank and cursed whenever he felt like it. I, on the other hand, was a sheltered, well-behaved young woman who dated sheltered, well-behaved young men. That pattern came to a halt when I met John Ball -- not for me, but for <u>him</u>.

We dated off and on for four or five months, and I broke it off with Randal. I learned that John had picked me out of the crowd at the beginning of spring quarter as I stood in line with friends waiting to register for classes in the old college gym. He and his friends were propped up in chairs among the trees watching the procession of girls as we made our way inside to register, bragging to each other about which ones they could ask out. He claims he made the decision then and there to turn his life around and become a better person. And he chose me that day in the registration line to help him make it happen. If I had known then what I found out after our first date, I probably would not have stuck around, but I didn't know, and I really liked this older guy. He told me he was a junior, having transferred in from Georgia Tech. Ha! So much for becoming a better person! He even altered his name a little bit, claiming he was called John, but his full name was Jonathan Andrew Ball. Not true. Neither was the part about being a junior. He had enrolled at Georgia Tech, but had failed all but one subject his first quarter, probably because he rarely attended class. He was asked to vacate the Tech premises, worked for a while, got into a bit of legal trouble in Atlanta (yet another story), and landed in Carrollton as a freshman at West Georgia.

As for turning his life around, that part did work its way to being true -- after a while. John was a gentleman at all times and treated me with respect. He even started going to class and cut

WAY down on his drinking and cursing. We had a great time together and fell in love. On our Christmas date in 1965, John suggested I open the glove compartment in his car to see what my present was. It was a small package, and I knew I would find a small velvet box inside. I was thrilled and so was he, so much so that neither of us can remember if he ever proposed. I just said yes! My only problem was telling my parents and my sister that I was going to marry a man five years older than I and a year older than JoEllen. To their credit, my parents just smiled and said if that was going to make me happy, then they were all for it. JoEllen, however, balked a little because of his age, but of course, she came around too before long. And we have, mostly, lived happily ever after.

CPSIA information can be obtained
at www.ICGtesting.com
Printed in the USA
FSHW020810251021
85617FS